Calling all dads and future dads—
On Being a Good Dad
is chock-full of everything you need to know
to be the father you want to be.

Len Kageler zeroes in on such sensitive and not-so-commonly discussed issues as:

- **Doomed From Day One**—When your own father was a poor role model
- **Kids Who Aren't Very Likable**—What to do if you love your kids... but don't really *like* them
- **Raised to Be a Macho Man**—Challenging society's warped image of what a man should be
- **The Wounded Father**—When your hopes and dreams for your kids are dashed to smithereens
- **Going Nowhere but Very Fast**—When the rat race steals precious time away from your family

In these pages you'll find practical help, solid hope, and godly healing for growing both as a father—and as a man.

By Len Kageler

Teen Shaping: Solving the Discipline Dilemma
On Being a Good Dad
Helping Your Teenager Cope With Peer Pressure
The Youth Minister's Survival Guide
Discipleship for High School Teens
Short Steps With the Lord

On Being A Good Dad

Len Kageler

Fleming H. Revell
A Division of Baker Book House
Grand Rapids, Michigan 49506

Unless otherwise identified, Scripture is from the Holy Bible, New International Version. Copyright © 1973, 1978, 1984 International Bible Society. Used by permission of Zondervan Bible Publishers.

Scripture identified NAS is from the New American Standard Bible, © The Lockman Foundation 1960, 1962, 1963, 1968, 1971, 1972, 1973, 1975, 1977.

Material from *Teen Shaping* by Len Kageler copyright © 1990 by Leonard M. Kageler. Used by permission of Fleming H. Revell Company.

Excerpt from *How to Raise a Successful Daughter* by Nicky Marone copyright © 1988. Used by permission of McGraw-Hill, Inc.

Chart on page 111 reprinted with permission © *American Demographics*, November 1990.

Material from "Self-Esteem in the Long Run" by Ronald Hutchcraft reprinted from *Parents and Teenagers* by Jay Kesler with Ronald Beers, eds. Published by Victor Books, © 1984, SP Publications, Inc., Wheaton, IL 60187.

Material from *Keeping Your Teen in Touch With God* by Bob Laurent © 1988, used with permission by David C. Cook Publishing Company. Available at your local Christian bookstore.

Library of Congress Cataloging-in-Publication Data

Kageler, Len.
    On being a good dad / Len Kageler.
        p.   cm.
    ISBN 0-8007-5427-1
      1. Fathers—Religious life.   2. Fatherhood (Christian theology)
    I. Title.
    BV4846.K34   1992
    248.8'421—dc20   91-36638
                                                        CIP

Copyright © 1992 by Leonard M. Kageler
Published by Fleming H. Revell
a division of Baker Book House Company
P.O. Box 6287, Grand Rapids, MI 49516-6287

Second printing, December 1992

Printed in the United States of America

To my own father,
Melvin G. Kageler,
With love and appreciation

Contents

Part IV   Outside Help

Michael Douglas

ON BEING A GOOD DAD

Part I

What We Are Up Against

Being a Man Today

I never gave fathering much thought—well, serious thought, anyway—until the social worker delivered Peter to our basement apartment door. It was a gray winter day, and Peter was ten days old.

My wife and I had agreed to have foster babies in our home as a kind of prenatal prelude to having children of our own. What a wonderful way, we thought, to prepare for the joys and rigors of parenthood. Three months later, Peter left for another family. Frankly, it was a relief.

Our friends had warned us that we would grow to love him so much we couldn't bear to give him up. Yes, we did miss him, but it sure was nice to have life return to normal.

Normal didn't last long, however. Rachel, also just ten days old, was delivered to us four weeks later.

I never gave the word *colic* much thought until this little bundle of agitated energy came to live with us. She cried constantly, was upset by the slightest disturbance, and from day one had her own distinct opinions as to how her universe should be arranged.

I remember trying to relax in the living room while Rachel was screaming in her crib down the hall. My wife had found an excuse to be gone for the afternoon, and I was left in charge. I stubbornly believed that one should not react to bad behavior (crying) with a reward (picking up and cuddling). Rachel cried, and I "relaxed" until she fell asleep exhausted. The woman upstairs, who could hear the commotion as loud and clear as I could, just about lost her mind. It required every bit of self-control she could marshal to keep from bursting into our apartment and scooping that child into her comforting embrace.

Rachel was with us less than two months. I missed her when she was gone, but once again I breathed a sigh of relief that life had returned to normal.

You may find this hard to believe, but after these two less-than-positive experiences, my wife and I *still* had children of our own. Our firstborn was a little girl. Would you believe that, three months after she was born, I secretly wished the social worker would come, as before, and take her away? How wonderful it would have been to have a normal night's sleep! This wasn't how I was supposed to feel, was it? It seemed I had come to the plate and struck out. Fortunately, I've done some growing since those first faltering attempts at fathering.

That little girl is not so little anymore . . . she's a teenager, and she has two younger sisters soon to enter teendom. If I lose sleep these days, it's not because of crying in the crib, that's for sure.

I'm a father. So are you. Usually I like it, occasionally I don't. What have we signed up for? What does it mean to be a father today? What does it mean to be a Christian man today? How in the world can we juggle the pressures of our careers and other responsibilities with the responsibility of being a good dad?

Help and Hope

This is a book of practical help and solid hope.

We need *help* because fatherhood counts. If we are too lenient with our children, they'll grow up feeling insecure. If our kids take insecurity into their teenage years, they will be ripe for a fall into the wrong crowd.

What is the most accepting group on a high school campus? It is not the Christians, the sportsy crowd, the brains, or the musicians. No. It's the "heavy metal rocker" crowd. All you have to do to be accepted in that group is to adhere to the dress code, listen to their music, and at least occasionally make a selection off the current menu of wild or illegal activities. Do that, and you're in! A great many insecure young people make that sad choice.

On the opposite end of the scale, being too strict can be toxic to children as well. Especially if you have a strong-willed child, a heavy-handed approach will almost guarantee major crises and rebellion during the teenage years.

How we relate to our kids as dads will impact their future in other ways too. It will go a long way in determining whether or not our daughters engage in premarital sex. It will heavily influence our sons' attitudes about females. Will our kids be happily married? Our relationship with them as children counts there too. Yes, our ability to be good fathers matters!

Even more basic, we all need help because most men are not born to be good fathers. Doesn't it fry you sometimes that so many females seem to naturally make good mothers? I know girls in our church youth group who, even at age fifteen, are excited about becoming mothers. They think about it often and have already made a few purchases to put in the hope chest for eventual use in a baby's room. Have you ever met a teenage boy who even had a hope chest? Ever met a teenage boy who was really excited about nurturing a baby? Ever met a teenage boy who had already done some shopping for the newborn he'd hold ten years later? I've been in youth ministry over two decades, and I've NEVER MET EVEN ONE.

Yes, in most cases, we males of the species have to learn to be fathers and learn even more to be *good* fathers. In this book, we're going to see that a good father (1) knows what he's up against, (2) knows he's not alone, and (3) knows his job as a dad. On this simple foundation we will build principles and insights. We'll look over the shoulders of men who are excellent fathers. We'll also look over the shoulders of men who are, or were, terrible fathers. We will learn, and try to grow, as we seek to understand how Christ working in us can bring positive change to our lives as men and as fathers. We'll see, in a deeper way, what help there is for us in The Book.

Here's where the *hope* comes in. Most of us are not perfect and occasionally that lack of perfection shows in how we handle parenting. We have tasted frustration, and it doesn't taste good. We live busy, pressured, and stressed lives, and success seems slippery. We're being pulled in a zillion directions at once. We see the efforts of others at fathering. Some make mistakes and their families seem okay. Others, we notice, make the same mistakes, and their families have the ambiance of a war zone.

No matter what the past, no matter how bad things have gotten, no matter how unlikely improvement may seem, it is *never* too late to improve as a dad.

We'll get insight from research, case studies, and personal examples. More important, however, we'll get hope from the One who gave us life and the gift of being a father in the first place.

So, we're aiming for help and hope in this book, but *not* guilt. Yes, all of us have made mistakes in the past, and some of us are paying for those mistakes now. We cannot go back and change the past, so all we are left with is the now. By God's grace and His work in our lives, we can intentionally change the present. The future will unfold differently as a result.

The State of Men and Fathers Today

Meet two fathers. Larry is in his early thirties and has a three-year-old son and a five-year-old daughter. He loves his wife and is a mid-level manager in the district office of a large corporation. When he comes home, his kids run to greet him. He scoops them up in his arms before the front door even closes. He can hardly wait to change his clothes, because when he reemerges from the bedroom, it's wrestlemania time. His wife chuckles as she hears squeals of laughter from the family room. After supper, Larry loves to play outside with the kids, pushing them on the swings, chasing them around the elm trees, and playing catch.

Larry is a very busy man. By 7:30 P.M. he's off to a meeting at church or the office, but his kids know Dad cares. They adore him. They're secure. There is no doubt in those little minds that Dad thinks they're the best. Larry likes being a dad and would, if pressed, modestly rate himself pretty high on parenting.

Meet dad number two. Jim is close to forty but doesn't feel it. He loves his wife, his job as an electrical engineer, and his home. When he comes through the door, he and his kids, ages seven and ten, say polite hellos. He greets his wife, who usually gets home from work an hour before he does, and turns on the TV to catch the financial news on CNN. At supper, his main conversation with the kids has to do with their performance. Scores on homework papers, first or second string on the team, practice time for music lessons—these are the concerns he raises with his kids. If one gets a B, he wants to know why it wasn't an A. If one makes two hits in a baseball game, he says it should have been three. He is quick to criticize and slow, very slow, to praise.

After supper, Jim reads the paper and heads out the door for a run. After a shower, he pulls his laptop computer out of his briefcase and sets it next to the phone modem and fax machine.

For the next two hours he does his banking, sends electronic mail to others in the computer network, and works on reports for the office.

Jim likes being a dad and takes pride in the achievements of his growing children. His kids love him too, but their insecurity increases as the months and years go by. Jim's wife sees the stress on their faces as Dad starts his nightly rundown of performance questions over supper.

North America has quite a few Larrys and quite a few more Jims. What do the researchers tell us about fatherhood in our society? It's not a pretty picture.

Time: The Bottom Line

A stellar researcher on the subject of fatherhood is Michael Lamb of the University of Utah. He has conducted large-scale studies, especially on the subject of father/mother interaction with children. All interaction is not the same, and he focuses on three levels:

1. Actual interaction (direct talking, playing together, and so on).
2. Accessible interaction (dad and child are not necessarily doing something together, but dad is available, as when dad is watching football and son is playing outside).
3. Ultimate responsibility: Which parent is in charge of making the decisions about child-care issues?

Lamb's findings? Fathers spent 80 percent less time than mothers at Level One, 67 percent less time than mothers at Level Two, and have virtually no Level Three responsibility. What about mothers who are employed outside the home twenty–forty hours per week? The statistics change only negligibly.[1]

What little time fathers spend with their kids is reduced as the children grow, though not as much with sons as with daughters.[2] Sixty percent of fathers do not desire to spend more time with their kids, and of the forty percent who do, seventy percent of them have wives who stand against more father involvement with the kids! Why would a mother be against her husband's increased involvement with the kids? She considers him incompetent and she doesn't want the power dynamics in the home to be messed with.[3]

A man may resist spending time with his children because he sees his babbling boy or drooling daughter as a barrier to marital happiness.[4]

How much time a father spends with his children is influenced by his income and education. Blue-collar workers tend to see themselves as the breadwinners of the home and disciplinarians of the children. White-collar fathers define their roles more broadly.[5] These dads, though still not nearly as involved as the mothers, are 30 percent more involved than similar fathers were in the mid-sixties.[6]

On the positive side, one study showed that the more a man was involved with his children, the better he felt about how things were going in the family.[7]

Men Leave Their Children Very Easily

The University of Pennsylvania's "Disappearing American Father" tells the sad truth of how readily men walk away from their families.[8] About 50 percent of children who do not live with their fathers have not seen them in the previous year. Not even once! Following a divorce, only 5 percent of the children see their fathers regularly during the following ten years. What is so painful for kids is this: They eventually realize their fathers *chose* not to be involved with them. Seeing children may bring back painful memories for a dad, and in some cases distance may prevent regular visitation, yet the father is *gone*. Right or wrong, kids take it personally.

It is not only internal pain a child experiences when a dad leaves; every aspect of life is touched. When a man leaves the family, his standard of living experiences a 42 percent rise, while the mother left with the children experiences a 73 percent drop in hers.[9]

Meet Heather Davis of Arizona. She is sixteen, lives alone with her mom, goes to school full time, and works thirty-six hours a week at a fast-food restaurant. Wait, there's more: "When my mom comes home from work every night I have dinner cooked and the house cleaned. On weekends, I sleep until I go to work. I'd rather sleep than go out with friends. Sometimes I get so tired of hearing I have to be responsible. I have too much responsibility for someone who's only sixteen."[10]

After Work: Leftovers

With the increased stress and pressure fathers feel at work, admittedly it is hard to give fatherhood much priority. In North America, England, and Australia, the average male in a white-collar job works over fifty hours a week.[11] According to kids, a large portion of fathers (37 percent) normally come home from work at the end of the day very grumpy.[12]

Are you in any of these statistics? I sure am. As a pastor, my work week is never below fifty hours, and sometimes when I come home at the end of the day, dealing with the emotional needs of my children is the last thing I want to do. I'm still in a recovery mode from the disasters of the day. A friend of mine had a little speech he commonly gave when he came home after a bad day. As soon as he walked in the door he announced, "It's been a bad day. Don't talk to me. Don't ask me anything. Don't even come near me. Just leave me alone for an hour and maybe then I'll be civil again."

Has it always been this hard to be a father? Did our fathers and grandfathers feel the same stresses? If things have changed, why? If being a father today is like coming to the plate with the bases loaded at the bottom of the ninth, it may help to understand how the game has been played up until now.

How Things Have Changed

My father and yours, my grandfather and yours, did not feel the same pressures to parent well that we feel. James Dobson asked his own father, "Do you remember worrying about me when I was a kid? Did you think about all the things that could go wrong as I came through the adolescent years? How did you feel about these pressures associated with being a father?"

Dobson reports his dad was embarrassed by these questions and answered hesitantly, "Honestly, I never really gave that a thought."[13]

The climate our fathers and their fathers were raised in was much more concerned with survival and the basics. From the late nineteenth century until the early 1960s, the father's role in the home was primarily that of breadwinner. Along with this economic role, he also was the main ambassador of the family to the outside world, as well as the disciplinarian.

Why didn't fathers, especially prior to World War II, have to worry much about their kids? Lots of reasons!

If they lived on farms, dads and kids, especially sons, had much time together working. There was no time for delinquency—too much work to be done. Both sons and daughters could readily see the value of their work to the welfare of the family.

Whether in a rural setting or even good-sized town, relatives were everywhere. "Gosh, if I did that, my Uncle Bob would kill me!" The extended family held children and young people in a sticky web of behavior expectations.

In small towns, news about a kid, especially bad news, traveled faster than fax. Children knew morning misbehavior at school would be known by mom before they got home that afternoon.

World War II changed the country forever. When the GIs returned from the war, they moved their brides to the addresses they had seen. Boys from the Bronx moved to Bellingham, Washington. GIs from Georgia wanted the big-city life of Chicago. California colonels were drawn to the cotton field country of Tennessee.

Then came the baby boom, a twenty-year demographic tidal wave of children born between 1945 and 1966. So many of these kids were born hundreds or thousands of miles from their grandparents. They were born in the cities, not the country or the small towns. When that high tide of children washed up to the school systems around the country, everything got big: big schools, big institutions. News no longer traveled back to mom and dad faster and fax. No one could even remember your name, let alone your parents. Baby boom children were raised by breadwinning fathers. We baby boom fathers recognize we must do more.

We can see that our kids need more than a roof and hot meals. Our fathers and their fathers could easily see they were needed to help provide for the family. Our kids certainly don't feel that need. Not many sons go out to milk the cows anymore. Not many daughters help with the canning these days. The food comes from the store, the cleaning lady comes regularly, and life, it seems, could get along fine without them. Fathers are needed to participate more with their kids, to help give them meaning and affirmation in an unkind world. The extended family and close-knit community, that sticky web of primary social relationships, is gone. Since the early seventies, the perceived role of father has shifted. He is still a breadwinner, but he is more than that: a nurturer. Our children will always be reminded that there are kids who are better-looking, more athletic, smarter, and more popular. At home they need a dad who can take the time to help them see they are worth something, they have value.

Many dads see this need, and that is why we feel the pressure. That's why things are different now. We know we need help in figuring out this thing called fathering. We want to succeed and yet the task seems almost too much. We voluntarily add to this pressure the drive to be more "successful" than our own fathers financially as well as in fathering.

In this chapter, we have seen that we are up against the pressure of time and perhaps our own incompetence or inborn lack of attachment to children. Also, we are raising our kids in a social context that doesn't provide the support and accountability that existed just two generations ago. In the next chapter, we turn our attention to one more item on the list aligned against us. But here's where we can hit that bases-loaded home run . . . because "Greater is He that is in us than he that is in the world" (see 1 John 4:4).

Questions for Discussion

(At the end of each chapter you will find questions to stretch you in your fathering. You can use these questions either in the setting of a men's group or as you read this book by yourself. But make sure you give yourself enough time to answer the questions carefully.)

1.   What was your father like? Was his primary role that of
      breadwinner, while your mother was the care giver?

2.   What was your grandfather like? What was his relation-
      ship with your dad and with you?

3.   The author states a big pressure against being a good dad
      today is time. In what ways do you feel this pressure?

4.   When your children were first born, what were some of
      your hopes and fears?

5.   Open your Bible to Jude 24. What encouragement does
      this promise give you as you think about what it means to
      be a Christian father?

Idea Corner 1

(At the end of each chapter you will find practical suggestions,
graded for three age levels, to help you apply the ideas of the
chapter to your family and to yourself as a father.)

With Preschoolers

Some sheets or blankets and clothespins will provide the raw
materials for a variety of creative tent structures. From the basic
sheet-over-the-card-table model, expand your undercover world
as space and imagination allow.

With Elementary Age

As a way to make Scripture come alive, as well as to identify
with the handicap of blindness, have a "blind supper" one night.
You and your son or daughter must wear blindfolds the whole

meal. No one else in the family is allowed to pass you the food. Talk about your feelings and frustrations at not being able to see. After you finish, and before the mess is even cleaned up, turn in your Bible to Luke 18:35–43. What feelings do you think the man had when he regained his sight?

With Teenagers

At an unpressured time for both you and your teenager, sit by his or her bed and listen to a song or two together on his favorite radio station. Have him explain the song to you if you don't understand the words. Why does he like or dislike the song? Does he agree with the perspective on life the lyrics present? How do the lyrics match up with Christian values? (Be sure not to preach if the song is terrible. Let your son or daughter begin to draw his or her own conclusions.)

2

So Just What Is a Good Dad?

Do you know anyone who is devoted to sports? I am, at least to one sport. How about you? Sports devotion is something most of us men understand. Sports devotion, in a strange way, can help us get a grip on being devoted to God and being a good father too. So what sport am I devoted to? You'll know in thirty seconds.

This year, my neighborhood really went to the dogs. No—it wasn't because of increasing crime or traffic. The city didn't build a garbage incinerator down the block, nor did a witches' coven move in behind the back fence. No one has been granted a license to run a kennel, either.

My neighborhood has gone to the dogs, or more properly spelled, D-A-W-G-S, because at this writing I live only three blocks from the University of Washington, home of the University of Washington Huskies football team. Every day, this huge campus comes alive as fifty-five thousand students, staff, and faculty fill its buildings, parking lots, and greenbelts. My family and I live right on what is known as "Greek Row," the street with most of the fraternity and sorority houses. We have a good-sized old house just a block and a half down the street from the last frat. We moved from the suburbs to this pulsating city within a city in 1986.

This neighborhood has gone to the Dawgs because recently the Huskies won another Rose Bowl. My street is already berserk enough during a normal football season, but Dawg Fever climbed through the season and peaked on New Year's weekend.

There are a lot of devoted Husky fans in Seattle. The stadium has seventy-five thousand seats, and most of them are sold out a year ahead to season ticket holders. They slog through the fog and rain as happily as they do sunshine to watch their beloved Dawgs perform.

I'll confess . . . I love football. I love the Huskies, but I love the Seattle Seahawks even more. I'm not a fanatic, mind you (although my wife may beg to differ with that assertion). But I do love to love this team. I know who the players are and something about most of them. I begin reading about them as soon as articles start appearing on the sports page. I have a good feel for the strengths and weaknesses of our team, as well as the other teams in the AFC West. My heart soars when we make it to the play-offs and sinks when we don't. I am discipling my daughters into an understanding of the game—play by play, rule by rule. If game time conflicts with a meeting at church, I cancel the meeting. Just kidding! I set the VCR to tape it, of course.

Football interests me. I give it my time and some of my focused energy.

Though this devotion to football occasionally frustrates my wife, she is glad I'm not devoted to all sports. College basketball begins to draw my gaze only the weekend before the Final Four. Pro basketball doesn't interest me until halfway through the play-offs. (It seems to me that almost all of the teams make it to the play-offs anyway, so I start paying attention about halfway.)

Baseball—now please don't be offended—is a real yawner to me.

I try to go to one Seattle Mariners game per year. To me, it's like a civic duty on the same level as voting. Most years, I bring a good book or the evening paper along to read during the game. Hey . . . at least I'm there and paid my money to support the team. This year, I didn't even bring a book to the game, a real gesture of enthusiasm on my part.

My friend Scott is the exact opposite. He loathes football but is a textbook case, an archetype, a paradigm of what it means to be devoted to baseball. He plays it with religious fervor. He watches it with rapt attention. It seems to me he knows everything there is to know about everything when it comes to the game and *all* the players on *all* the teams.

Are you devoted to sports? Perhaps it's bowling, golf, tennis, World Federation "wrestling," hockey, soccer, or basketball. If you're devoted, you know it. You know how it affects your life. You think about it, you study it, you like it, you talk with others about it, and it takes your time.

Through this excursion into the world of sports devotion, we can catch an insight into a crucial key to fathering. I am totally convinced that we will never succeed at fatherhood unless we are devoted to it, and we'll never be properly devoted to fathering unless we are devoted to Jesus Christ with the same or even more fervor than my neighbor is devoted to baseball and I am devoted to football.

By what measure are we to gauge success in our lives and in fatherhood? Our devotion, our real, tangible, heart-interest devotion to Christ is our only and first source when it comes to success in life and success in fathering. This approach to life is a radical departure from success as it is defined by the world. It is a radical departure from success even as it is defined by those who call themselves Christians, but whose commitment is on a par with my tepid feelings about Mariner baseball. How do we learn to be devoted to Christ and our children? Pardon the return to sports jargon, but the answer in both cases is the same: The best defense is a good offense.

A Good Offense for Spiritual Life

Here are three steps—an offensive strategy—in becoming more devoted to the Man Jesus Christ and His working in our lives. Remember, this it the foundation for all devotion to family and learning to father well. Remember too, when we use the word *devotion*, we are not talking about a squashy, pale, vapid, weak-spined religious term that reminds us of stained-glass saints enshrined in medieval cathedrals. By *devotion*, we mean something rock solid. We're talking about a commitment that will affect our lives. It is a commitment that will affect our thinking, our reading, our inner interest, and how we spend our time.

Step One: Admitting the Need

Yes, this is about as basic as it gets. The first step in improving our spiritual life is admitting that we need to and want to make the change.

A good start in this process is to simply pray that God will show us our own need and create in us a deep desire for improvement. This was the attitude of David when he scratched these lines:

Search me, O God, and know my heart;
test me and know my anxious thoughts.
See if there is any offensive way in me,
and lead me in the way everlasting.
                                        Psalm 139:23, 24

If you have this foundation of your life all figured out, great! If, however, your spiritual life is not as solid as it needs to be, here is a good place to begin. If you're not even sure you want to be highly devoted to Him, back up even a step further and *pray that you'll want to want* to have a vital relationship with Him!

This process may be uncomfortable, even painful. Like children tightly grasping a piece of chocolate, if we don't learn to let go, the very thing we grasp will melt away and be gone.

I've been a Christian since age seven and have been a pastor since 1975, and God is still exposing areas of my life in which my grip needs to be loosened. My spiritual life is kind of like a warped board: just when I think I've got everything nailed down tight, *pop*, up comes a corner that needs to be nailed down again. The areas God shows me to put back into proper perspective are not wrong per se. It is usually a matter of good versus best, not good versus bad.

Sometimes the issue is *loving God more than things.* I recall the first time God invaded my awareness about possessions. It was my freshman year at the University of Washington and I had a brand-new Camaro. My dad and I had ordered it the spring before, and it arrived the week the new cars came to the showrooms in the fall. I was one proud boy! I was living in a Christian fraternity house, and I often parked the car in front of the dining room window so we could all "enjoy" seeing it while we ate. There was a Christian sorority next door. Think of the social implications of having a new car! I had a whole houseful of girls to impress, and I went at it with gusto. Of course, I also showed devotion to my car by washing it nearly every day and inviting my new friends to go for rides.

A few weeks into the quarter, the Camaro was parked around the corner. One of the guys came in while I was eating lunch.

"Hey, Len, I just saw your car. What happened to it?"

I dropped the spoon into my chicken noodle soup. "What do you mean, 'What happened to it?' "

"You haven't seen it? Better go look!"

I was gone faster than Spock disappears in the transporter room of the Starship *Enterprise*. I reappeared outside and there it was—the driver's side was dented from rear to front.

"A drunk frat boy with an old truck, no doubt," I mused. No note on the window. No evidence I could find to nail this crime to a drunken, careless, guilty, sideswiping twenty-year-old.

Through this ego "crisis" I felt God saying to me, "Look, Len, I was nice enough to give you the new car, but for goodness sake, don't let it go to your head! Cars are fine, but don't love them more than Me—got it?" Well, I tried to "get it" and to keep that lesson a learned one down through the years. Have I always succeeded? Of course not. The "things" have varied—the acreage in the country, the big house in the right part of town, the new computer—but God still reminds me when my devotion to things begins to crowd out my devotion to Him.

Another area revealing our tight grip on life is that of *loving others more than God* . This is a hard one too. People are real; we can see our wives, we can touch our children. The sad fact is, though, if we love people more than God and build our lives accordingly, we are setting ourselves up for major league pain.

As a pastor, I have the unhappy opportunity to see people hurt people. The amount of human wreckage that washes up to my office door sometimes boggles my mind.

I've seen the hurt in a father's eyes. For years he worked so hard to afford the big house on the country estate. His dream had come true. The land was large enough so each of his three grown sons could have three acres. He planned that each would build a home there with their wives and children. What a kinship paradise this would be: loving sons with wonderful daughters-in-law, and grandchildren laughing and playing all around. This decades-long paradise dream was vaporized in a few short weeks as one by one the sons firmly told their dad they had no intention of moving to his acreage—then or ever.

Yes, we are to love our wives and our children, yet our mental grip on them had better be loose or we are headed for a fall. There is nothing wrong with love and care for the people God gives us, but we must remember that here today doesn't mean here tomorrow.

William came home to a house that felt strangely different. His attention was drawn to the kitchen table, to the note from Delores, his wonderful wife of ten years: "Dear Bill, I've been doing a lot of thinking lately. You've been too busy to notice . . . normal. You are an abusive tormentor. You will hear from my attorney within a few days." William had no clue his wife was unhappy!

Paul and Denise were reading the Saturday paper on the back-yard deck. It was a glorious spring morning. Denise noticed the patrol car drive down the street but went back to the editorial she was reading. The doorbell rang. She and Paul looked up and saw the car parked in their driveway. They walked around to the front of their home. As they approached the two officers, Paul noticed one had a badge that said "chaplain."

"Are you the parents of Mary Stall?"

Denise's eyes widened with horror. "I'm sorry to have to tell you that your daughter Mary died about an hour ago out on Interstate 405. She was ejected from the car in the crash and died of head injuries just as the medic unit arrived. There was nothing they could do to save her."

Walking with husbands, wives, and parents through the grief process is the most difficult thing I've ever been called on to do. Some never seem to regain their footing. The relational rug has been yanked out from under them, their world has collapsed, and they refuse to do anything but drift through the motions of life thereafter.

Some go through the usual grief but then life, hope, and growth go on. Their life foundation was not a human being.

They weren't banking on a person to never fail or leave them. After the rubble settles around their broken world, there they are, still standing tall, ready to dust themselves off and walk on in faith. The crisis reveals they loved God more than they loved others.

I stood next to Steve as his brain-dead daughter lay on the hospital bed before us. She was "alive" medically, but only from the neck down. Steve had had more than his share of tragedy in the last five years. His first wife died of cancer. His second wife died in a car crash. Now this. He hadn't eaten in twenty hours, so we left the hospital to get something.

"I try to remember to focus on her gain, not my loss."

What could I say? This wonderful Christian girl had been laughing and joking two days before—confident that she was in God's hands as she faced this very risky surgery. We all were happy with the news that the surgery went well. Ten hours later, though, like a set of dominoes falling, one by one things started to malfunction inside her. It took only a few minutes for an emergency team of specialists to assemble, ready to operate again, but it was too late. For all practical purposes, Jill was dead.

I took Steve back to the hospital. That evening, Jill was pronounced dead. Steve grieved, of course, but recovered and is living a life of purpose and joy in God's power. Again it was clear to all around him: he had built his life on a Rock, not sand.

Perhaps we have no problem with loving God more than others or more than things, but another warped board that sometimes pops up is the issue of *loving God more than self*. Loving Him more than self shows itself when God and His Kingdom figure into our planning. It shows itself when we are more concerned for His reputation than ours. It reveals itself when our choices in life do not evidence enhancement of our own power, prestige, and glory. We show faithful willingness to do the little things, the humble things, to serve God and people. We let Him take care of our reputation and position in life.

The first step of a good offense in learning devotion to God is to admit our need and begin praying that God will work in us to make a change.

Step Two: Practice

I am committed to a lifelong learning process of gaining new skills. People start fossilizing when they stop learning new things. Author Howard Hendricks says, "If you stop growing today, you stop teaching tomorrow . . . I MUST keep growing and changing."[1]

I decided when my big 4-0 birthday came, it was time to learn to play the piano. A musical basket case since childhood, I considered this venture in the same category as the "Star Trek" byline, bravely going where no man had gone before. I discovered one thing fast: To learn to play the piano requires *practice*. There are no shortcuts.

The principle of practice applies to spiritual devotion too. Devotion to God can't be purchased at a fast-food chain. It is not microwavable and ready to live in twenty seconds. A heart for God can't be franchised and sold like Service Master or McDonald's.

Of course, books abound on how to gain and live the Christian life. There is one idea that has helped many Christians switch from a Christian life of struggle and failure to one of consistent winning. Here it is: It is totally impossible to live the Christian life on our own power, period. No man possesses the discipline, consistency, and fortitude to live out all the Bible requires. Therefore, our only hope is to let go and let God do what He has wanted to do all along: live through us. I used to pray, "Lord, help me be a better Christian. Help me live for You and be more patient, understanding, and on and on." I began to pray instead, "Lord, I'm all Yours . . . live through me, enjoy Yourself through me today. I am weak and I know it. You are strong, and I look forward to seeing what You're going to be up to today."

Apparently, the Apostle Paul had learned something similar as he stated, " 'My grace is sufficient for you, for my power is made perfect in weakness.' Therefore I will boast all the more gladly about my weaknesses, so that Christ's power may rest on me . . . For when I am weak, then I am strong" (2 Corinthians 12:9, 10).[2]

How does a man practice this truth? Take this little quiz, for starters. Rate yourself on a scale of 1–10, 10 meaning you strongly agree with the statement.

I Am a Good Model to My Family and Others . . .

_____ 1. In being a loving person.

_____ 2. In being joyful.

_____ 3. In having a peaceful spirit.

_____ 4. In patience.

_____ 5. In being able to endure hardship.

_____ 6. In being kind and thoughtful.

_____ 7. In having self-control and avoiding impulsiveness.

_____ 8. When it comes to anger management.

_____ 9. In being humble, not haughty or proud.

_____ 10. When it comes to not being fearful.

_____ 11. In spending quality time with God daily (or nearly every day), in speaking to God (prayer), listening to God (Bible reading), and worship.

Next, choose an area that needs work. For example, maybe number 8, anger management, is a problem. Your kid leaves the garage door open, doesn't do a chore right, or talks too long on the phone, and you blast him off the planet. How often does this happen in a normal week? Five times? Twenty times? Twice? Whatever the number, cut it in half, for starters, and pray.

DON'T PRAY: "Lord, help me not be so angry with John and Sue this week." Sorry, it won't work. Asking God to help us after we've done our darnedest doesn't lead to happy endings.

DO PRAY: "Lord, I have a problem. I get so angry with my kids, and though they probably deserve to be yelled at much of the time, I realize my anger isn't solving anything. Lord, I'm weak . . . I can't change this on my own. Please, God, I want to step aside and let You live through me on this one. I want to be so close to You that Your Spirit will give me a different response. I might not have enough faith to believe this will all be solved next week, so I'm believing that instead of six blowups, You'll keep me down to three. Maybe I've got enough faith for that. Lord, I'm all Yours."

Have some quality time with God every day before going to work or while commuting to work. Make that your prayer. See what happens. Visualize a situation in the coming week where you anticipate a blowup might occur. Think about and pray for an alternative response. Visualize the correct way of handling it. It will take practice, but as the Holy Spirit begins to rewire your response mechanism, you will see practical progress. You are, in fact, learning to be devoted and show devotion to God.

Also, either in your head or out loud, sing. Choose to be Spirit-filled by giving thanks and singing praise to God. Having a thankful and singing heart won't change your circumstances: your boss may still be unreasonable and hard to please. Your strong-willed daughter may still be in rebellion. But having a thankful and song-filled heart helps you deal with tough issues with a more peaceful spirit than you would otherwise.

Step Three: Being Accountable

In football, the players work as a team. If everyone does his job well, winning becomes the norm. We can win when it comes to learning devotion to God if we make sure we're part of a team. It is at the core of a good offense, spiritually. How?

We need to be part of a group that holds us accountable. It can be a small group Bible study or "care ring"; it could be a men's weekly breakfast; ideally, it can be with our spouses. We need a relational environment where we can be open, honest, and vulnerable. We need a place where it is okay to say, "You know, I yell at my kids at least six times a week. God only knows how much I want this warfare to stop in our family. Would you pray that next week my anger response will be cut down to three times instead of six?"

It is amazing how accountability motivates us to change. Recently, I studied the cases of 175 youth pastors who had been fired. Some of them lost their jobs because of money mishandling. A lot of money from fund-raisers, retreats, and the like passes through a youth pastor's office. Some churches require the church treasurer to balance the youth group's checkbook every month. In these cases, the youth pastor knows he is accountable—and this, if nothing else, mandates proper money handling.[3]

If we need to cut our in-house angry outbursts by 50 percent, knowing we will have to give a report in just seven days will make a difference.

Again, our accountability "group" could be our wives, one close friend, or a small group.

This three-step offensive strategy of (1) admitting the need, (2) practice, and (3) accountability will work to help us learn the solid devotion to God that we want. The same three steps will trigger devotion to our families as well.

A Good Offense for Fatherhood

Devotion to sports . . . it comes pretty easily. Devotion to God . . . we can learn it and make real progress. Devotion to our children . . . we can learn this too, but for some of us it is hard. Why? We easily give our energies elsewhere.

An immense amount of academic energy has been aimed at the issue of what motivates men. One researcher put it this way: "Work comes to be seen as men's principal *family* role; they are the 'breadwinners' or 'providers,' with the fruits of their work portrayed as their major contributions to their families. . . . Men supposedly succeed in their family roles by what they do *outside and away from* their families."[4]

We saw in chapter 1 that men are realizing it is not as easy to raise a family now as it was two generations ago. The risks are greater, so there is a felt need to be more involved. The trend is definitely toward a greater *desire* to be involved with the family. A recent study by *Gentlemen's Quarterly* magazine, a publication not exactly noted for its Christian values, revealed that 84 percent of the men they surveyed felt family was *the* most important part of their lives.[5] Even among eighteen- to twenty-four-year-olds, 64 percent said family was their most important life focus.[6]

We'll look at this in much more detail in chapter 6, because it is possible to learn to be a good father. After getting our act together spiritually, learning to be devoted to our children is the foundation on which the rest is built. Again, let's consider a three-step offensive strategy.

Step One: Admitting the Need

Perhaps devotion to your kids comes naturally to you and if so, be thankful. For the rest of us, it doesn't. We have to learn it and keep on learning it.

If you are normal, it doesn't take much to get you to admit you feel a need to be more devoted to being a good dad. That's why you're reading a book like this. Admitting the need should focus your prayer: "O Lord, work in me to make me more devoted to the children You've given me."

Step Two: Practice

How do we practice to increase our devotion to our children? *We need to practice wonder.* What does that mean?

There is a little sign by my computer screen at the office. Whenever I'm on-line, I can see that little sign with my right eye as I produce, by God's grace, the electronic paperwork of local church youth ministry. The sign says this:

Gifts to Give the People Around Me

- Wonder
- Enthusiasm
- Kindness
- Gratitude

I try to practice wonder in my life, at work and at home. Still wondering what it means to practice wonder?

Consider this: It is truly mind-boggling when we realize the specialness, complexity, and importance of the people around us. Let's focus on our children. Doesn't it fill you with wonder to watch them grow up? At each stage, there is something amazing to watch. Let's do a quick tour of the growth highlights our children demonstrate.

Newborns   So much happens so fast in the opening weeks of a new life! Watch the newborn's eyes begin to track your face or your finger. Feel the strength in the grip of that tiny hand. Put your ear on that soft chest and hear, really hear, that new life pulsating inside. Lay your baby on your chest and feel the strength and regularity of his breathing. Fall over backward in surprise when that little guy or that little girl flashes you the first smile or you hear the first laugh. There is a person in there! Be amazed at what is going on. It is wonderful!

Toddlers   Oh, my goodness, when little Johnny or little Sally starts walking, watch out. It's exploration time! See the wonder in his eyes as he makes his own choices as to where to walk, what to play with, who to go with. Hear the first words and sentences, evidence of ongoing cerebral wire-laying in that young head.

Twos and Threes   Now little Johnny or Sally has opinions as to how the universe should be arranged, right? Where did those opinions come from? Does someone put self-will pills in the baby food or the ice cream? Wherever it comes from, it is another event to step back and wonder about. This little person is beginning to have an identity and he or she is trying to communicate these first strong preferences.

Fours and Fives   Wonder at the delight in playmates and play. Watch your five-year-old play with a friend. Listen to the story line and hear the fantasy life. Listen to expanding vocabulary. Be amazed at the ability to think.

My wife and I almost passed out when our daughter Carolyn, at age five, called me on a parent power play. I wanted to do yard work uninterrupted. She wanted to play outside, be with me, and specifically wanted to know *when* she could come out. I told her, "Carolyn, you can come out when I'm half done." Her response (at high volume): "I can't know when a half is until I know what the whole is!"

Six- to Ten-Year-Olds   This is a huge chronological chunk, and it is filled with wonder possibilities. Our kids really learn about their world. They are in school and experiencing the won-

der of reading and learning how things work. Wonder as they
invite Christ into their lives and evidence sincere devotion to
Him and a desire to do the right thing. Take them to Disneyland
if you can and enjoy the look in their eyes as they experience the
Magic Kingdom.

Eleven- to Thirteen-Year-Olds   In this stage, there is enough to
be amazed at to fill a closet with diaries. Do your kids have a huge
need to sleep in on Saturday mornings? Can they just barely
scrape themselves out of bed Sunday mornings to come to
church? If so, they are right on schedule as their bodies start
growing up and out. All this growth is lots of work, and a body
needs to sleep in once in a while to recoup. Does your twelve-
year-old run into things? It's a great sign of growth—the brain
hasn't got a good fix on the exact current whereabouts of feet,
shoulders, fingers, and legs.

Fourteen- to Sixteen-Year-Olds   Wonder at the complexities of
the middle adolescent world. Enjoy their questions and searching
. . . it's time to begin to figure out their place in the world and
the future they can begin to see. Marvel at their ability to re-
cover from disappointment and setback. Yes, unrequited love,
lost money, lost friends, failed free throws, and missed goals are
all tragedies at the time. Yet somehow, teens learn that life goes
on and God still cares.

Seventeen- to Nineteen-Year-Olds   Ready or not, they are
wanting to fly. The energy and focus young people this age can
give to the goals they have is amazing. They are figuring out that
this thing called life is *serious business,* and they had better get
their acts together. Young men and women this age have a huge
capacity for empathy, care, and concern. Watching them choosing to love and choosing to care can make us sit back and thank
God for the budding maturity we see. More exciting yet is it

when they choose to aim some of that love and care toward their fathers.

You might be thinking, *Hey, there's a down side in each age group too. In fact, I know fathers who almost hate their kids because there has been so much rebellion and struggle.* You're right. We've got dirty diapers to deal with at one end and perhaps a foul-mouthed, ungrateful almost-adult at the other. Yet I believe that, as we practice wonder at each stage, we make it more likely the next stage will be good.

Kids are masters at picking up nonverbal cues. I know many teenagers who turned out to be disasters because it was exactly what their parents expected. One Christian father told me, "Raising teenagers is a miserable experience, and don't let anyone tell you different." It didn't surprise me. This father had been dreading teendom for years, and his stormy forecasts all came true.

On the other hand, for years my wife and I have been totally excited about the coming teen years. All the joy and all the fun we envisioned is happening. We have two early adolescents and one middle adolescent—supposedly the worst stages. We even have one who is a classic Dobson *Parenting Isn't for Cowards* very strong-willed kid, but wow, we're having a great time. As a father, I've built a behavioral pattern of practicing wonder and enjoyment of my growing kids. They know I'm devoted to them.

Step Three: Accountability

The third step in developing a good offensive strategy to be more devoted is simple. We can have the same small group talked about earlier hold us accountable for practicing kid-inspired wonder. Each week, we should be responsible to say something wonderful about each of our kids. As we do, heartfelt devotion to fathering will begin to spread through our thoughts and actions.

*   *   *

So what is a good father? A good dad is one who is learning to be devoted to Jesus Christ. A good dad is one who is learning to be devoted to his kids. We can begin to approach our Christian walk and our lives as fathers with the same fervor many men devote to the Final Four, the Super Bowl, or the World Series.

It helps us to know we are not alone in this thing called fathering. There is much to learn from the disasters and successes of others. Let's look over some famous and infamous shoulders to see what we can see.

Questions for Discussion

1.   The author talks about the importance of loving God more than (1) things, (2) others, and (3) self. Read Luke 14:26, 27, 33. Match each verse to one of these three. In which area do you need the most help right now?

2.   From the quiz on page 35, share two of the areas of your life where you are a good model to your family and others.

3.   From the same quiz, share two of the areas of your life you scored the worst in. What specifically can you pray for and be held accountable for in the coming week?

4.   What is *wonderful* about your kids right now?

Idea Corner 2

With Preschoolers

All that glitters is gold in the eyes of a child. A bottle of glitter, some glue, and lots of paper can make for a fun project.

Rip out pages of a coloring book and instead of coloring, glitter them. If weather allows, do this one outside, as glitter gets on clothes, floors, and wherever a glittered child wanders.

With Elementary Age

Take a tour with your kid. If you live in a town large enough to have a McDonald's, you live in a town that has a business that gives tours. Is your town or area famous for anything like turkeys, airplanes, cars, chocolate, or lawn mowers? Many firms gladly give tours. Make a few phone calls and take an afternoon for an inside look at how things are made.

With Teenagers

If you have a VCR, rent the movie *The Mission*. Set in the South American jungles of the eighteenth-century, it is the true story of one priest's calling to protect the native population from Spanish slave traders. It is appropriately rated PG, as the brutal violence of the slave traders is depicted realistically. Watch the movie together. What was good about the good guys and bad about the bad guys? What is your mission in life?

Part II

We Are Not Alone

Fathers in the Word

The *Washington Post* splashed it on the front page first. The *New York Times* treated readers to a series of reports and analyses. Like a rock dropped in a pond, the impact of this latest scandal-in-high-places story spread in the financial markets. The *Wall Street Journal* moralized that resignation was the only and best alternative. "A public show of incompetence and a blatant disregard for decency. . . ." Articles in the *Toronto Globe & Mail* along with the *London Times* implored the Congress to take leadership and chop off this limb before the disease infected other cabinet-level departments.

In embassies from Moscow to Tokyo, from Madrid to Johannesburg, Cabinet Secretary Thomas Williams became famous—or infamous—for mishandling his office. When Secretary Williams refused to step down, the bad press continued, from the *Times* to the tabloids. What were once Washington whispers became cries of outrage. Conflict of interest, using his office for private gain, and disregard for the law of the land . . . evidence mounted.

Secretary Williams had been in public service for over twenty years. He was a busy, totally dedicated, and tireless worker. He worked from 6:00 A.M. until 10:00 P.M. There were always people to see, calls to make, embassy parties to be seen at. Secretary Williams's two growing sons admired their father and the freedom his life-style gave them. His wife felt discipline was up to the father, so she said nothing as the boys grew out of control. Both the secretary and his wife were frequently out of town. Word began to spread in Washington that the Williams's home was a haven for teenagers who wanted to drink, try drugs, and gain sexual experience of any persuasion.

Then the *Washington Post* broke the story to the nation: The General Accounting Office was investigating expense account requests that were quadruple the norm. Secretary Williams denied the charges and affirmed his faith in his boys. Allegations and revelations avalanched over many months. While Mr. and Mrs. Williams were out of town, the boys hosted their own twenty-first birthday party, which became the standard by which future Washington wild parties would be measured.

Soon thereafter, Secretary Williams hired his two sons as consultants, employing them in his department and authorizing huge expense accounts. Even readers of the *National Enquirer,* no strangers to sensationalism, were aghast at the raucous, lavish, and orgiastic life-style its pages portrayed. Dad was a frequent visitor to his sons' posh apartment. The FBI began an investigation as allegations surfaced that Secretary Williams was financing all the luxury, not only at government expense but also through a circuitous paper trail that pointed to extortion and racketeering.

Do you remember Secretary Williams? I hope not, because this tragic but true story was not born in Washington. It was not actually scooped by the *Washington Post.* I changed the names and a few of the circumstances to protect the true identities until now.

The year: about 1100 B.C. The location: Shiloh, the main worship center of the confederation of tribes collectively known as the nation Israel. The sons' names: Hophni and Phinehas. The father: Eli, high priest of Shiloh. Their sad story litters the opening chapters of 1 Samuel in the Old Testament. The scandal, intrigue, cover-up, and international repercussions of this self-destructing family was truly front-page material.

The Bible is full of famous and infamous fathers. Unfortunately, fathers who failed spectacularly are more in evidence than those who succeeded.

You and I are not alone at this thing called fathering. Men have been challenged, frustrated, honored, and destroyed by their children down through the years. Let's look briefly at other fathers in the Bible. Then we'll think about how God is a Father to us and what the Bible specifically says to us as fathers. Finally, let's be encouraged with some practical help for becoming godly men.

More Headlines

One thing about the Bible: it's honest. It portrays real people with real problems. Information about men in the Bible was not screened by a media consultant, press agent, or campaign adviser prior to inclusion.

Consider Asa, father of Jehoshaphat, father of Jehoram, father of Ahaziah. Their world, the ninth century before Christ, may seem strange and distant to us. Distant or not, we can easily pick out both the thrill of victory and the agony of defeat in their lives. What kind of dad was King Asa? We don't know if he played ball with his son Jehoshaphat. We have no record of walks in the park or reading bedtime stories. We do have a record, though, of a man who was an excellent manager. He had, in executive parlance, vision. From the accounts in 2 Chronicles 14—16, we can deduce a forty-one-year series of good headlines in the local press.

This man was proactive: he made things happen in a way that brought unity, not conflict, both in his own country and in foreign affairs. Furthermore, he had a heart for God. He made some risky, potentially unpopular decisions based on his religious convictions. How easy would it be today, for example, for a president to shut down the tobacco industry? How well would it go over if the president crusaded to have any movie with a rating worse than PG-13 banned? Asa, believing the people needed specific spiritual guidance, shut down whole industries in his country. He closed the idol factories and idol worship centers, throwing many people out of work.

Asa was willing to take a risk for God, to stand up and take the heat for unpopular decisions. His son was watching closely. Asa's long political career was not without blemish, but Jehoshaphat picked up the best of his father's qualities. He proved himself an excellent chief executive during his twenty-five-year reign. His life is covered in 2 Chronicles 17—20 and, like his father's, evidences sincere and deep spiritual convictions. These convictions remained steady, despite mind-boggling increases in both his private fortune and the wealth of his country.

There were blemishes on Jehoshaphat's career as well, yet the Jerusalem press corp seem to have been favorable to the end. Unfortunately, personal integrity, leadership ability, and morality are not hereditary. We don't know how much time he spent with his children, or if he ever sought to carve out time from his busy schedule. Imagine trying to run a government without computers, phones, fax, or copy machines! Jehoshaphat eventually died, and everyone in his country, from the shadow of the palace to the Negev outback, mourned the passing of a leader who had become a legend in his own time.

Son Jehoram was handed the keys to the royal palace at age thirty-two. His first official act was to murder his seven brothers. It was a political statement: "I'm in charge, there are no rivals, and you can expect *real leadership* from me." One thing about Jehoram: he was never ambiguous. He never bothered with subtlety.

Six years into his eight-year reign, Jehoram received an unauthorized performance-appraisal review from a wild-eyed religious fanatic named Elijah. Elijah had a few observations, comparing him in a rather unfavorable light with his father and grandfather:

> Thus says the Lord God of your father David, "Because you have not walked in the ways of Jehoshaphat your father and the ways of Asa king of Judah . . . and have caused Judah and the inhabitants of Israel to play the harlot . . . and you have also killed your brothers, your own family, who were better than you, behold, the Lord is going to strike your people, your sons, your wives, and all your possessions with a great calamity; and you will suffer severe sickness, a disease of your bowels, until your bowels come out because of the sickness, day by day.
>
> 2 Chronicles 21:12–15 NAS

From that day forward, Jehoram's stock tumbled. At home and abroad, the press reported political, economic, and military setbacks. Two years later, Jehoram died an agonizing death as his bowels did, in fact, come out (2 Chronicles 21:19). We are told that no one in the whole country or international community mourned his passing from the scene. We aren't told why Jehoram turned out so bad when his father and grandfather were so good. Who came next? For better or worse, Jehoram had discipled one of his sons well.

Hearing the news of his dad's death, Ahaziah, age twenty-two, stormed into Jerusalem with the private army his generous allowance had funded. First on the slaughter agenda was every single one of his brothers. With this beginning, we don't need much imagination to fill in the rest of the story. Mercifully for the country, this punk king died of battle wounds only a year later.

The four fathers and sons spoken of here are a good sample of dads and offspring in the Bible. Some turn out good, some turn out bad. Generally the sons model the fathers, but not in every case. The writers of the Bible were not sociologists or family counselors. We are given only glimpses of family life and are left to draw many of our own conclusions.

We are left no such ambiguity when it comes to the ultimate Father described in the Bible, God Himself.

Number One Father

Think about it: the Bible, from beginning to end, tells us God is a Father. He is our Father, our Heavenly Father. How does this idea make you feel? Rate the feeling below (circle):

It leaves me cold   It makes me feel really good

1   2   3   4   5   6   7   8   9   10

Our response to the idea of God as our Father will largely come from our experiences with our own father. Was your dad kind, loving, caring, and always there for you? It is easy to love and worship God, right? Was your dad abusive, dictatorial, anger-filled, and sullen? If you find it hard to have warm feelings about God, you are normal.

Like watching a ship sinking in the distance, Tom's mother watched his dad swallowed up by an ocean of alcohol and gambling. He left just after Tom was born. He has never paid child support or alimony. To this day, at age thirty, Tom has great difficulty in feeling God's presence. His earthly father was absent nearly from day one. To Tom, God is absent too.

Sure, Tom's head tells him God is there—it says it in the Bible, right? But his heart sends a different message. He usually looks out on a universe from which most traces of God have vanished. He tries hard to feel God, but it's like trying to grab a fistful of sand. The harder he tries, the more it seems to slip between his fingers.

There are many Toms in North America, men whose conception of God has been critically damaged by fathers who majored in "Jerk" while in college. Overcoming this handicap is not easy, but it can be done. The steps to recovery involve recognition of the problem, its source, and honest dealing with the feelings involved. This is best done with a Christian counselor.

No matter what your earthly father was like, let's now look at how God comes across as Father in the Bible.

He Loves Completely

Is God a cosmic killjoy, just waiting for us to have a little fun so He can squash us flat with calamity? Hardly. Yes, bad things do happen to good people, about that there is no doubt, but God's loving heart comes through the Bible's pages again and again.

The Prophet Isaiah begins quoting God in father terms beginning in the second verse of chapter 1. It is later, though, that we feel God's loving heart for us:

When you pass through the waters, I will be with you; and
when you pass through the rivers, they will not sweep over
you. When you walk through the fire, you will not be burned;
the flames will not set you ablaze. . . . you are precious and
honored in my sight . . . because I love you. . . .

Isaiah 43:2–4

It is easy for us to read the words *I love you* and not give it a
second thought. The Old Testament was written in the Hebrew
language, and anyone who reads this text in Hebrew would not
breeze by this phrase without pause. There are several ways "I
love you" can be said, and this is the strongest, most intense, and
deepest usage of which the Hebrew language is capable.

Visualize a moonlit night, out by the oasis. Jacob and Rachel
are getting a little time to themselves, as they often do in their
fourteen long years of courtship. (Their story is found in Genesis
29.) Jacob looks over into her beautiful eyes and, using the same
Hebrew words found in Isaiah 43, says, "I love you." Sweet
Rachel might have a cardiac arrest and fall backwards off her
camel into the sand! It just doesn't get any better than this when
it comes to love in the Hebrew language.

God, our Father, loves us.

He Is Faithful

American fathers come and go. As we have already seen in
chapter 1, they leave their children and spouses with such ease
it is shocking. Tony Campolo once counseled a dad who was
about to leave his family. Tony implored him to stay and work
things out. The man refused and added with self-satisfied equiv-
ocation, "You don't expect me to sacrifice my happiness for my
wife and kids, do you?"[1]

God isn't like this.

"Never will I leave you; never will I forsake you" (Hebrews 13:5).

Jesus referred to God as His Father and our Father nearly two hundred times in the Gospels. We know that Jesus is God the Son and is the visible expression of God to us (Colossians 1:15). Jesus said to His disciples and to us who are believers, "I am with you always, to the very end of the age" (Matthew 28:20).

No One Outgives God

Those who seek God and make Him a priority find God's fathering of us to be that of generosity. We see His provision, often undeserved on our part, and we feel like resounding with the Psalmist, "How can I repay the Lord for all his goodness to me?" (Psalm 116:12).

He Pays Attention to Us

Many a son or daughter is frustrated by a father who doesn't listen. The son or daughter is telling with enthusiasm about the high points of the day, and the father grunts over the newspaper without even looking up in response.

God doesn't grunt at us over the latest issue of *Heaven Today*. He is always aware, always tuned into our thoughts and heart cries. This one was high up on David's list of favorite things about God.

"I love the Lord, for he heard my voice; he heard my cry for mercy. Because he turned his ear to me, I will call on him as long as I live" (Psalm 116:1, 2).

He Accepts Us

I was an only child. My dad dreamed of watching his boy play Little League baseball and junior high football. Unfortunately, I had zero interest in playing sports at the time but finally agreed to turn out for football in eighth grade. After four days of miserable torture, humiliation, and confusion, I quit the team. My dad was very disappointed, but I knew he still accepted me.[2]

Jesus told the parable, an earthly story with a heavenly meaning, about the prodigal son. Here (Luke 15) is a picture of how God accepts and receives us, even if we choose to do our own thing.[3]

So God is portrayed as a loving Father in Scripture. He is our number-one and ultimate example of how it is to be done. We have much more than this specifically about fathering in the Bible. Let's take a look at one subject about which there is some controversy and confusion. The Bible says a good father disciplines his kids, right? What, really, does this mean?

A Bible and Father Sampler: Discipline

We cannot read the Old Testament without seeing that, for the Israelites, education without tears was no education at all. In Deuteronomy, it is advised that the rebellious son should be stoned to death (21:18–21). Fathers flogging their sons was part of normal life (2 Samuel 7:14; 1 Kings 12:11).

In the Book of Proverbs, we find the fullest Old Testament "Doctrine of Discipline" as it relates to the family. Here is a quick tour:

The father who spares the rod hates his child (13:24). Lack of this kind of discipline could lead to death (19:18). Discipline is administered by the rod (22:15, 23:13, 14). The rod imparts wisdom (29:15), and discipline promotes a healthy family life (29:17).

Based on these Scriptures and trying to apply them, many Christian fathers have taken a heavy-handed approach in correcting and disciplining their sons and daughters. It's a closed case, right? Unfortunately, unhappy statistics are beginning to emerge about how much physical abuse has gone on in Christian families. Youth workers and teachers are becoming aware of the telltale signs that signal an abusive situation in the home.

The Bible does not teach that we are to hit our kids. It does not teach that we as fathers have the right to lord it over our young people and force their compliance with our every wish. Parents who use this approach generally see rebellion as the fruit of their disciplining efforts. They not only see rebellion but they also experience frustration themselves. If the Bible says this is the way we're suppose to do it, why doesn't it work?

If it doesn't work, the answer should be obvious: Perhaps God didn't mean the Book of Proverbs to be the final word when it comes to how a parent is to treat a son or daughter.

I invite you to listen in on a conversation I had that begins to explain what I mean:

Mark: Len, you believe fathers need to really be strict with their kids, don't you? I mean, it's the parent's God-given role to punish, and there are so many Scriptures that support this. "Spare the rod, spoil the child!"

Len: I'll answer that, but first let me make a comment. Mark, I'm very surprised you don't believe in heaven!

Mark: What?

Len: What I mean is that many Bible doctrines are revealed progressively through Scripture . . . in other words, you don't get the whole story until you get into the New Testament. Heaven is a great example. There is no heaven in the Old Testament, or at least you've got to be pretty creative to find it there. So, should we fixate there and not believe in heaven? Of course not, because we've got the whole picture in the New Testament.

Mark: Are there other examples?

Len: There are many more. Of course, the whole doctrine of salvation is filled out in the New Testament. So is the doctrine of the church. So is the subject of the end times. And Mark, *so is the subject of discipline!*

Mark: I don't hear anyone out there teaching that!

Len: I strongly believe that, while the Old Testament gives us good reasons for discipline, it is from the New Testament that we are to draw our cures for actual living of life. The method and motive of father to child cannot, should not, be heavy-handed punishment. *Love and kindness are to be the driving forces within the family as Christian support group.* How did Jesus generally treat His disciples or others who needed discipline? Think about it! I recognize fathers must discipline their kids, but we must take our cues not solely from what we get in Proverbs.

The Example of Jesus

As Christians, we are wanting to be "in Christ," to let His life be demonstrated in our day-to-day living. It should be of interest, then, how Jesus handled situations where those around Him deserved some discipline. Jesus was showing His disciples what a loving father is like. Let's look at a few examples in the Book of Matthew to see how He managed the disciples in some of their bad moments:

When Peter rebuked Jesus for talking in terms of being a suffering Servant, Jesus rebuked him quickly and then turned the situation into a teaching opportunity for all of the disciples (Matthew 16:23ff).

Jesus was in a bad mood after seeing so much unbelief among the people of His day. His disciples had failed to heal a little boy, yet He took the time to teach them patiently (Matthew 17:14–21).

The disciples seemed to be quite concerned about who was the best. Jesus doesn't put them down or blow them away. Instead, He called a little child to come and stand in front of them. "You want to be a leader? Be like a child" (*see* Matthew 18:1–4).

A mother of two disciples made an outlandish request of the Master, and He questioned these two about their understanding of His mission. The other ten disciples were miffed by the request, yet Jesus did not publicly humiliate them but instead tried to teach all of them about what true power and authority is (Matthew 20:20–28).

In these few chapters of the first Gospel, we readily see that Jesus' approach to His disciples was not heavy-handed. Yes, He guided and corrected them, but with a view to teaching them. And this is exactly what discipline is: it is one way we teach our young people.

Key Verses for Fathers

Granted, we are not Jesus, and our young people are not the disciples—even if we have twelve of them! According to Paul, there is to be a mutual commitment in the Christian family between parent and young person. The young person is to obey the parent, but the father is not to provoke the son or daughter. "Provoking," according to Ephesians 6:4 and Colossians 3:21, results in anger and discouragement on the part of the young person.

This is a good example of progressive revelation in Scripture. We'll have to look very hard for material in the Old Testament to find concern that a young person might be discouraged or angered by the actions of a parent. But here, in the New Testament, where a family is composed of Christians, there is to be Christlikeness toward one another. There is a distinct concern for the young person. Parents are admonished in Ephesians 6:4 to bring up kids in the discipline and instruction of the Lord. Yet now this discipline is to be done with a definite acknowledgment on the part of the parent that discipline could harm the young person—and in the Christian home, that harm is to be avoided. How?

The Family as Christian Support Group

If Christian family members are to behave in a Christian manner toward one another, then anything in the New Testament that tells us how to relate to one another applies in the home.

If Christian fathers are to be servants of the Lord, any correcting that is to be done, whether inside or outside the home, is to be done in gentleness (2 Timothy 2:25). Paul acknowledges that our gentle approach gives the other person the space to come to repentance and know the truth.

A quick trip through the Sermon on the Mount (Matthew 5—7) humbles us all when we try to apply it with respect to dealing with our young people. We are to be meek (5:5), have mercy (5:7), and be peacemakers (5:9). We are to settle our differences in love and without anger (5:21–25). There is to be no revenge seeking, but instead, if we are wronged, it is appropriate to turn the other cheek (5:38, 39). A judgmental and critical spirit is not appropriate either (7:1–5).

Of course (and you knew this was coming, didn't you?), we are to show the fruit of the Spirit in our fathering. Paul is not compartmentalizing the believer into behaviors that are appropriate inside the home and other behaviors for outside the home. If we are believers, and the Holy Spirit is functioning through our lives, then this wonderful fruit (love, joy, peace, etc.) should be in evidence no matter where we are—even in the home. Even after a hard day at the office. Even when the car breaks down. Even when we've got a sore throat. Even when we've had a bad day.

Impossible? Of course it is, and that is the beauty of the Christian life, whether at home or away from home. As explained in chapter 2, it is supposed to be impossible, because then the only realistic alternative we have is to step aside and let

Christ do what He was wanted to do all along: live through us completely.

The fruit of the Spirit doesn't come as we grit our teeth and try our best. It comes not as a result of determined effort. It comes as a result of being in love with Jesus Christ and seeking Him most of all.

As we think of our Christian life and fathering in these terms, we set the stage well for the guiding and correcting of our young people to be done in His kind of love.

But you know, fathering with the presence and power of the Lord in our lives doesn't happen automatically. We have looked at fathers in the Bible, we've considered *the* Father in the Bible, and we have taken one bite-size sample of the Bible's teaching for fathers. Before plunging ahead, we must think about how we, as harried, hassled, and hurried men, can manage to spend time in The Book.[4]

Learning to Find the Time

There is no magic, no secret formula, to make it work. Success doesn't require years of academic study or an advanced degree. No certification, licensing, or permits are required. Most men who enjoy consistent and quality time alone with God and are getting good input from the Bible have two basic things in common: (1) they have set a time and (2) they have agreed to be accountable. Yes, theoretically it is possible to have a good devotional life without these two, but there aren't many men who do—at least I haven't met them.

Time and Place

Find a man who can tell you his normal time and place for his devotional life and you have found a man who is succeeding spiritually.

My grandfather, a gentleman farmer, had his time and place. No matter what was happening with the family or who was visiting in the house, at 9:00 P.M. he went to his chair in the dining room, got out his Bible, and read. He was in bed by 9:30 and up at dawn to do the morning chores.

Most of us can only relate to one piece of that schedule: up at dawn or before. At the other end of the day, we fall into our beds exhausted at 11:00 P.M. or midnight. Crammed in between is work and the commute (ten to twelve hours), eating, bills to pay, meetings to attend, phone calls to make, and other various and assorted interests we pursue. The number-one excuse for a substandard or zero devotional life is that we are too busy.

Here's the rub: we are very successful at finding time for the things we really want to do. My neighbor is a very busy executive who frequently travels. There is always time for racquetball, however. I've always got time to watch some football, even if I've taped the game and see it late. Others always have time for golf, tennis, or TV.

Time alone with God will always fail if it is just a duty, another thing to do on our long and onerous list. In chapter 2, we talked about learning to be devoted to Him. We talked about developing an offensive strategy for our spiritual lives. As we grow more deeply in love with Him, our *wanting* to spend time with Him will increase, until we want it bad enough to name a daily time and place.

I know many men who have a great time with God during the morning commute. They pray as they drive (eyes open, of course) and listen to portions of Scripture via cassette tape. A great time with God can be had on public transit too. I've seen Bible readers on New York subways, Chicago trains, Denver airplanes, and Vancouver, B.C., buses. Sure, this may not be as ideal as sitting home alone in a quiet room with no distractions. Some men have this, and for them it's great. God is happy, though, to make home, car, bus, or even bike a sanctuary.

I enjoy praying on the run—literally. Long-distance running is how I stay in shape. People wonder how I manage to scrape myself out of bed at 5:15 three mornings a week and run. It's not boring at all. The longer I run, the more time I have for prayer. On runs longer than six miles, I bring along verses of Scripture on little cards to memorize and think about.

The "A" Word Again: Accountability

My walk with God got a big boost when Janet and I got married. We agreed to be accountable to each other for our devotional lives. At the end of the day, we report to each other what we read out of the Bible and what we got out of it. Simple, short, but very effective.

Many men join a weekly or twice-monthly Bible study or support group. We answer questions about a passage during the week and report our answers in a small group. Whatever type of group, the outcome is the same: if we know we're going to be sharing with others in our small group about our Christian life next week, we are motivated to have something to say. There's nothing mysterious about it.

We can learn to be a father in the Word. As we do, we realize we're not alone. The Holy Spirit is in our lives to work, change, encourage, and strengthen us.

We have looked over the shoulders of a few fathers of the Bible. Let's continue to learn as we look for ways fathering should or should not be done.

Questions for Discussion

1. Can you think of any other examples of good or bad fathers in the Bible?

2. How does the idea of God as your Father make you feel? Share and explain your score from page 52.

3. Which of the aspects of God's fatherhood appeal to you the most and why? Look up the Scripture referenced. How does this make you feel?

4. Which of the father characteristics of God do you need to better show to your own children?

5. What is the time and place for your devotional life? If you don't have any, share what you think would be a good plan.

Idea Corner 3

With Preschoolers

Remember blowing bubbles as a kid? Chances are, you recall a small jar of bubble solution and a little plastic blower. That was yesterday. Today's bubble-blowing possibilities are boggling. Paraphernalia comes in a wide assortment of shapes and sizes, allowing children to create huge and multifaceted bubbles. Do this in a park, and in a while you're bound to have spectators. There's just something about bubbles in the air that fascinates children of all ages.

With Elementary Age

Your son or daughter is old enough now to understand that there are hurting and hungry people in the world. Go grocery shopping and bring a bagful of food to the local gospel mission or food bank. Don't rush off. Get a feel for who goes there and what is done with the food.

With Teenagers

During the summer, or at another time of the year when there is little academic pressure for your son or daughter, take a night class together at a community college. Learn a new skill together: photography, computer graphics, calligraphy. Shorter-term classes of all sorts are offered at community centers or through the public libraries. Pick something you would both find enjoyable and interesting.

4

Famous and Infamous
Fathers of the Past

I hate plumbing, but not as much as I used to.

I know some men who can do anything and everything when it comes to home repair. Add a circuit breaker for the new hot tub? They can do it, no problem. Fix the washing machine motor? Sure, it's easy. Troubleshoot a noisy furnace fan? Just the bearings, right? Well, if my wife had been shopping for a mister-do-it-all husband she failed, and failed with gusto. I'm afraid of our breaker panel. Appliance motors and machines are mysteries. Any whisper of discontent from the furnace sends me to the yellow pages.

Don't get me wrong. I'm not against personal involvement in these things. Before I'll attempt a home repair, though, I need to be shown what to do. Call it discipleship, call it apprenticing, call it whatever you want: if you show me, I'll try to learn.

As I said, I hate plumbing, but I'm making progress. In that regard, recently I have experienced both the thrill of victory and the agony of defeat. My wife and I are blessed with a home that was built in 1913. Some of the plumbing has been updated, but most hasn't.

A clogged upstairs bathtub drain prompted the usual application of household unclogger, but to no avail. Loathing to phone a Roto-Rooter man, I marched to the hardware store and asked for the strongest stuff in stock.

"Be careful," the clerk said, "sulfuric acid is dangerous."

At home, I donned enough protective gear to qualify for a nuclear reactor cleanup and confidently applied my sulfuric acid. It worked! Unfortunately, it worked so well that it ate right through the seals of several old pipes. Leaking? Too kind a description. *Gushing* is more accurate. Acid and water coming forth from hitherto unimagined places, soon to leak down to the kitchen below.

I called the plumber, *fast*. One hundred thirty-four dollars later, my problems were solved.

Four weeks passed, and we had another plumbing puzzle to ponder: water from the wall behind the washing machine in the basement. I called the plumber *first* this time. Fifty dollars into his visit, he said, "Here it is!" And yessiree, there it was: a visible crack at the joining of a copper pipe to a lead pipe. He calmly explained that to fix it he would have to tear out the whole north basement wall, remove all lead pipe, and replace it with copper. The job would take awhile and cost a thousand, maybe two thousand dollars. I let that thought roll around in my head awhile and asked if there were any other choices.

"Well, you can try silicone seal and wrapping it with something."

Bingo, I said to myself.

I thanked him, paid him, and went to work.

My father-in-law had shown me how to wrap a cracked pipe with silicone seal from a tube with strips of aluminum foil. I did it, just as he had shown me. It held, and I think it's going to hold for a long, long time.

The only reason I could do it was that I had been shown how. It's the same way with fathering. We are obviously not alone as dads. There have been millions of fathers in the past, and there are millions of fathers on the planet right now. When we first get into fathering, we do so with no previous experience. Yet we can know a lot about fathering from learning how others have done it. Let's take a glance backward in time and see what we can see.

German Fire

Never has a single act of vandalism so changed the world as the morning that a German monk defaced the door of the cathedral at Wittenberg. As darkness turned to dawn on October 31, 1517, people gathered around that great door to read it for themselves: ninety-five alleged errors of the Catholic Church, signed by someone named Martin Luther.

The reformation he triggered became known as the "Protestant Reformation" because those involved were *protesting* problems in the church with the purpose of *reforming* the wrongs they saw. As the movement blazed its way across Germany and Europe, it was more than doctrine that was reformed. Luther and the Reformation consciously tried to elevate society's view of marriage and family life.

It wasn't easy. Forty percent of adult women were single and nearly fifty percent of the children died before reaching age five.[1] One Reformation pastor mentioned the low regard of marriage and family by sermonizing, "Having seen how much effort, anxiety, pain, need, care, and work are involved in marriage, they [men] would not recommend it to a dog, and to save their children from it, they gave them over to the Devil by forcing them into the cloister."[2] It's true. Many fathers turned their kids over to the church at age five. This doubly beneficial practice let fathers get rid of children, and it provided virtual slave labor for the church.

Reformation pulpits began to encourage fathers to actively care for their children, and after a child was age six, the father was to have the dominant role of parenting.[3] A good father was to protect his family, care for them, and not ruin himself with alcoholism. Though spanking was on the menu selection for discipline, it was not to be a first choice. Physical abuse was condemned.[4]

At the center of all this social revolution in the midst of doctrinal revolution was Martin Luther himself. In spite of the burden, stress, and time pressure of turning Europe upside down, Martin Luther was a great dad!

Luther's five children, Hans, Lenchen, Martin, Paul, and Margaret, knew their father was the most famous man in Europe. But they also knew their dad loved them. Every evening he spent time with them, playing, singing, and goofing around before they went to bed.[5]

Usually the Luthers had an extra fifteen to twenty people for dinner every night—important people with impressive titles from important places. Yet these people saw a man committed to his family, who loved to laugh and joke with them. They saw one who took the time to be a dad, no matter what the pressures and setbacks he experienced. They heard him pray for God's grace and strength to be in him, so he could better love his wife and kids. No wonder the Reformation improved the standing of marriage and family life!

Though we have no videotapes of Luther's parenting practices, we get the feel of what he was like. We may be tempted to feel that we are among the busiest, most pressured and stressed-filled men around. Someone like Luther can show us that, in the midst of being maxed out (how many of us have twenty guests for dinner every night, with visitors knocking daily from all corners of the civilized world?), we can still create a calm and a joyful shelter for our children. We can *be there* for them.

English Ice, English Thaw

Like a rock skipping over a pond, we jump ahead a full two centuries and splash down in Epworth, England, a tiny island on a vast sea of English peat. Epworth's main and only road was so muddy much of the year that people used stilts to get from place to place. We land in the manse of the Wesley family and find a family under fire.

The Reverend Samuel Wesley was the town's pastor. He was, as was the pastor before him and the pastor before him, about as welcome as smallpox. Yet Samuel Wesley hung in there, year after year, and fourteen of his children were born there. He stayed even though they torched his home. He stayed even though a murder attempt nearly succeeded. The Wesleys had an austere, difficult life in Epworth. Samuel Wesley made sure his children were organized, disciplined, and busy. Though not all of his children survived past childhood, none of those who did rebelled. Rebellion was a luxury that this family could ill afford. Everyone had a job to do, and each understood his or her contribution to the whole.

Samuel Wesley's fathering report card would have at least three As and one F:

> Building self-esteem: A
> Building responsibility: A
> Building respect for authority: A
> Leading his kids to Christ: F

It was not until 1727, at the age of twenty-four, that John and his brother Charles Wesley received Christ into their lives and had assurance of their salvation. Once these young men were converted, however, they amply proved that God plus one or two is a majority. Samuel Wesley had taught his boys many good things, but he had overlooked the most important.

A hundred years later, at the other end of England, no such lack could be found in the father of Lydia Mueller. George Mueller consciously, intentionally, and specifically taught her about a personal relationship with Christ. He wanted her to believe God was real and could be trusted for the miraculous. In their daily life, they looked for things that showed God was working. They believed God in impossible situations and expected Him to work. George had a policy of not telling anyone about the financial needs of the orphanages he had founded in Bristol, England. Yet, money came from the most unusual sources again and again. Clearly, God could be trusted to meet the needs of the ministry the Muellers had founded.

Lydia was thirteen when she smashed through a rare bout of self-pity and doubt that had come over her father. His orphanages were causing trouble on Wilson Street. His mind was heavy about moving the entire operation to an even worse area of the city. Lydia kindly informed him that it was God's will for him to build (not rent) orphanages not in the city but out in the country, where there was room to play and room to grow.[6]

In a flash, George realized it. His daughter was behaving exactly as she had been shown the last thirteen years. Got a problem? Nothing is too big for God. Pray. Believe. Act on faith. That was the life-style she had learned. Her faith gave him a toehold, and in the coming years, huge orphanages were built debt-free in exactly the country setting Lydia's faith envisioned.

Looking over Mueller's shoulder, we learn how to communicate *living* faith. He is a model of enthusiasm for God and a conscious sharing of prayer concerns and their answers.

American Steel

We next skip across the Atlantic and touch down in the teeming town of Chicago, where we find a very stubborn man accomplishing incredible things for God. D.L. Moody's own dad died when D.L. was four. He helped his mother the best he could while growing up, but by age sixteen, the little valley northwest of Boston, where he grew up, was a world much too confined. He left home, went to Boston, and found a job. For better or worse, D.L. was a young man determined to do his own thing, no matter what others thought.

What kind of dad would D.L. be? Well, his wife, Emma, got a clue a few days after their wedding. Despite her protests, D.L. marched off to preach to the Northern armies fighting the American Civil War. It was to be a pattern she would often see repeated. For Moody, it was God and ministry first. Wife and family would be a distant second.

Their first child was Emma, born in 1864, and then came a son, William, in 1869. One biographer couldn't help but notice D.L.'s lousy example when it came to fathering:

> . . . D.L. was a self-styled free-lance religious worker, rushing from one job to another. He worked for the YMCA, he spoke at Sunday school conventions. He was responsible for the Illinois Street Church. . . . For the next two or three years he was generally too busy to see much of his family.[7]

In 1870, supporters surprised the Moodys with a new house. The Moodys were very grateful, especially Mrs. Moody. Since D.L. was gone more than he was home, at least she had a comfortable place to be a single parent. Throughout D.L.'s life, he gave all his energy to his calling and his motto: "The world has yet to see what God can do with one man wholly committed to Him." Dwight and Emma had one more child, a son, in 1879.

How did growing up without much of a father affect the Moody kids? D.L. made a trip to England and met with George Mueller. Did Mueller help him see the importance of spending time with his children and consciously teaching them about an alive God? We don't know the answer to the second question, but we do know the answer to the first.

Emma, Will, and Paul Moody turned out great. All three became strong and active Christians. Both Will and Paul graduated from Yale, which was at the time an excellent Christian college. Will succeeded his dad at the Northfield Church and was there until his death in the 1930s. Paul became the president of Middlefield College and preached widely in revival meetings until his death in 1945. Emma married an administrator of Moody Bible Institute and evidenced deep dedication to God and His ministry until she died at age ninety-one in 1955.

What can we learn from D.L. Moody's fathering style? Can we zealously pursue our careers and assume our kids will turn out great? Though we might think yes when looking at the Moodys, we should not be too hasty. Another American man of Christian courage and steel, Albert Benjamin Simpson, fathered the same way but with a much different outcome.

A.B. Simpson did not intend to found another Protestant denomination. The year was 1877. An experienced pastor, A.B. Simpson had accepted the call of a prestigious Presbyterian church in New York City. The prim-and-proper pew fillers of his church were shocked and chagrined that A.B. preached to immigrants and began bringing them to church. He eventually resigned and, forsaking the financial security of the big church, rented a theater. He took an ad in the *New York Times* and asked people to come to hear his vision to reach the lost. The place was packed; expectations were high. After preaching his heart out, only seven people came forward to heed his call: an alliance of Christians committed to missions. From this unlikely beginning, the Christian & Missionary Alliance was born.

Simpson's wife had begged him not to move the family to New York, but as it was with Moody, so it was with Simpson: God and ministry first, period. He had already established a pattern of disregard for his family. Only a couple of years earlier, A.B., his wife, and four children were on a train. The kids were climbing the walls and out of control. Mrs. Simpson was desperately hoping her husband would help. Would he? No . . . it was time for him to pray. He walked to a part of the train where he would be away from the distraction of his crying kids and hapless wife.

In New York, Mrs. Simpson's worst fears became reality. Their oldest son, age thirteen at the time of the move, quickly succumbed to the seduction of city life. Gambling and alcoholism ruined this young man and finally killed him. At age thirty, his body could take no more. On his dying day, like the thief next to Jesus on crucifixion Friday, Albert, Jr., begged God for forgiveness.

Credit A.B. with this: the stress of seeing his son become a hardened young punk of the city made him change his parenting priorities. To the relief of his wife, he began to spend much more time at home. His ministry was in the city, and he could come home at the end of the afternoon to be with the kids before going out for an evening meeting.

The change came too late for the second oldest son, James Gordon. He was nine on moving day and followed his brother with gusto—even including a deathbed conversion at age thirty-seven. Three other children followed: Mabel, Margaret, and Howard. While not owning the vision of their father, they did manage to keep at least a semblance of Christianity in their lives.

We can see why taking our cues for successful fathering from someone like D.L. Moody could be a mistake. Simpson used the same approach with his first two kids, and they were disasters.

Seeing the offspring outcome of these two men illustrates both what researchers today have amply proved and what most parents know intuitively: kids are not all the same. A heavy-handed or absentee parenting pattern might be fine for one son or daughter. The same mistakes may trigger complete rebellion in another.[8]

Church history is replete with the sad stories of notable fathers who were too busy with Christian activities to spend time with their children.

Pioneer missionary William Carey and missionary-explorer David Livingstone placed the entire burden of parenting on their wives, and the pressures were greater than the women could bear. Evangelist Billy Sunday and his wife, Nelle, whom he called Ma, were a great evangelistic team. She was sometimes called General Fix-It by her family, but unfortunately she was unable to fix the deeper hurts of her family. The lives of the children were riddled by heartaches and tragedies. Undeniably these fathers were eminently used by God, but their own children bore the brunt of the fathers' callings.

In this century another father was becoming famous, not for a heart for God but for laughter. Imagine having Groucho Marx for a father. Arthur Marx did and tells all quite freely.[9]

Groucho was involved with his son from day one. He changed diapers and took his wife and preschool son everywhere he went to perform. Between performances, he would rush back to the hotel to give his wife a hand with Arthur. Home base eventually became Riverside Drive in New York City. Groucho often took his son to city parks and organized baseball games for Arthur and friends.[10]

Groucho was far from perfect. His marriage was stormy and he scoffed at religion. Arthur felt the stress of his parents' frequent uncoupling. Once, at age eight, he ran away. Walking five miles on a hot, muggy, New York afternoon is no small accomplishment for a little boy. As Arthur rested with his nose pressed to the plate glass of a soda shop, he heard a car drive up. His father rushed forward, asking, "What are you doing here?"

"Running away," Arthur replied.

"Do you have any money on you?" Groucho asked. Arthur shook his head.

"Here's a dollar," said Groucho, handing him a bill. "You can't run away without money."

With that, Groucho turned around and headed to the car![11]

The two of them laughed over that scene many times.

Arthur's adult life has seen repeated successes as a tennis player, playwright, and author. He is realistic about his father's shortcomings yet appreciative that his dad made him a high priority in his hectic career. *Son of Groucho* makes for absorbing reading.

Lessons from these good and bad examples of fathering are apparent. A father who spends time with his kids is likely to see those kids feel good about themselves and do well in life.

Remember, we are not alone as fathers. There is much to learn from watching others, just as I learned from watching my father-in-law fix a leaky pipe. Yet this brief backward glance may leave us unsatisfied. These men lived, and fathered, in the past. Their world was one without fax and freeways, computer and copy machines. Wouldn't it help to compare notes with busy fathers who have recently raised their kids or who are right now groping to figure it all out? Let's look at some real men and some real struggle.

Questions for Discussion

1. What are you like at the supper table after a particularly stress-filled day? How do you think Luther managed to have so much fun with his family despite the heavy pressures he faced?

2. Do your kids see God as alive or dead as they observe how you live your life?

3. Which of the fathers listed in this chapter are you most like? In what ways?

4. How do you react to A.B. Simpson's leaving his wife alone to cope with four wild kids while he went off to pray? Are you ever guilty of leaving your wife to be a single parent while you go off to something ostensibly more important?

5. Proverbs 22:6 says, "Train a child in the way he should go, and when he is old he will not turn from it." What is your understanding of this verse? Is it a promise to be claimed? Is it an illustration that you reap what you sow?

Idea Corner 4

With Preschoolers

Ready for a hilarious few minutes that requires no equipment and only the ability to bend over? Stand up, spread your legs, and invite your kid to crawl or run through your legs. One catch: the tickle monster might wake up, and you know what tickle

monsters love to do . . . tickle little kids! Pretend to be asleep for
their first few passes, then come to life.

With Elementary Age

Most parents prefer that their children not grow up to be
"heavy metal rockers," a music style that implies a life-style of
sex, alcohol, and drugs. You can kill curiosity and shock them
into an anti-heavy metal music stance by doing this: Show them
part of a heavy metal concert. If your town has a music festival
that includes a heavy metal concert, go, if just for fifteen minutes.

No festival? Mill around in the crowd outside a coliseum or
concert hall where a big-name heavy metal concert is about to
happen. The ambiance of the crowd will give your kids the
creeps.

No crowd to mill around? Rent a heavy metal concert video
from your local video outlet. After doing one of these three, ask
questions like these: How did being around these people or seeing these people make you feel? Do you want to be like them
when you grow up? Do you think these things make Jesus happy
or sad? Why?

With Teenagers

At an unpressured time for your teenager, sit down and compare notes on the subject of friendship. What does your daughter
(or son) look for in a friend? Have her describe what she likes
and dislikes about her friends. Has she had any disappointments
with friends in recent months? How would her friend describe
her? Tell her about your friendship struggles at the same age.
Who are your friends now and why?

Real Men, Real Struggle

We can see we are not alone as fathers. We have looked at fathers in the Word and some famous fathers of the last four hundred years. Now I invite you to join me in a tour of some American fathers today. Some are very famous men, others are famous only to their families and colleagues. I take you on this tour because I don't hate plumbing as much as I used to. Remember the story in chapter 4? I learned from my father-in-law. We can learn from other men today just by listening to them.

As I interviewed or researched these men, I asked five questions. Not everyone answered all five, but most did. Before we begin the tour, answer the questions yourself:

1. What are you up against as a dad?
2. What is helping you learn to be a better father?
3. What is one frustration you are facing as a father?
4. What is one success you feel you are having?
5. In one sentence, what is your job as a dad?

Marvin Businius
Occupation: Church Growth Consultant
Kids: One, Age Eight

Marv's job involves travel, and lots of it. Before his daughter, Jannell, was in school, she and his wife frequently went along. Now, the challenge to be a good dad looms large, yet Marv feels good about what he sees in his growing daughter's life.

What roadblock is he constantly up against?

"I feel my own personal limitations keep me from being the father I could be. Combine that with how difficult it is to make for quality time, and it's tough. I travel so much that what time I do have at home really has to count."

Marv recounted a frustration he's working through right now.

"I'm trying to figure out how to teach Jannell to do the right thing without taking away her initiative. Just yesterday, she and I went out to water the tomatoes she had planted in the garden. She was fascinated by how fast the water came out of the hose nozzle and just about blasted the plants out of the ground. I tried to show her how to water in a more gentle manner. Her priority, though, was clearly to have fun with the water, not concern for our tomato crop. My wife was watching from the kitchen window. Without hearing our conversation, she could see I was getting frustrated. I was trying so hard to encourage Jannell yet she was blasting those poor tomato plants into the next county."

Marv smiled as he talked about a success.

"She is becoming a very caring, open, and sensitive young lady. She's really clued into my own ups and downs as a dad, and she does what she can to encourage me. I see her doing this with others too, and it really makes me happy."

What about things that have helped him learn to be a better father?

"Reading. We subscribed to *The Growing Child* newsletter from Purdue University.[1] Though not a specifically Christian publication, it helped me understand what was going on developmentally, and it gave us ideas for family projects and things my wife and I could do practically to make our family life better. I highly recommend it. I know there are many good books about parenting, but this newsletter was concise, crisp, easy to read, and easy to use."

What does he see as his main job as a father?

"To model Christlikeness. I want to show her authentic Christian living. This year I had the joy of praying with Jannell and hearing her receive Christ into her life. That's been the biggest joy for me so far as a dad."

Tony Campolo
Occupation: Sociologist
Kids: One, Career Age

The other day, Tony and I were talking about fatherhood over lunch and . . . just kidding. I haven't talked to Tony, but I have listened in on him and his son, Bart, discussing their relationship. *Things We Wish We'd Said* is an intimate look at a father-son friendship. Have you ever wondered what kind of family events pleased and provoked a high-profile author/speaker/thinker like Tony Campolo?

Can you guess what his chief roadblock to being a better father was?

Time. Tony traveled extensively, taught, wrote, and was a man in demand during most of Bart's upbringing. Looking back on it, Tony wishes he could have given one whole day a week just to be with his family.

Reflecting on this struggle echoed by other church workers, Tony remarks, "Never once have I heard a minister say that he wished that he had spent less time with his family and more time on the work of the church. That should tell us a thing or two."[2]

As for frustrations and regrets, there are more than a few.

Tony regrets not having led his son to Christ. Bart became a Christian while a sophomore in high school through a soccer friend named Joel. Being such a high-profile Christian, and knowing other sons of other famous Christians who had left their faith long ago, Tony was afraid of coming on too strong.

Another big frustration was battling the world's values and their impact on his son. One day Tony discovered his fifth-grade son's "people cards." The high-status in-crowd of the school produced baseball-card-like fact sheets on other members of their class. The card included an unkind pencil drawing, various good and bad points, and an overall desirability rating. Tony was dumbfounded when he discovered his son was a card-carrying member of this snob group.

How about successes? It is hard not to smile at the honesty here. Bart writes, "Whatever else you may have failed to do, Dad, you succeeded in making me believe without a doubt that I was the most essentially wonderful person you had ever laid your eyes on and that anyone who failed to recognize my inestimable value was simply oblivious to the obvious. You made me absolutely sure of myself. And that, more than anything else, has made all the difference in my life."[3]

Both Bart and Tony enjoyed the fun times and the traveling together. Trips to the poor in the Dominican Republic helped Bart understand the world is not such a pretty place. This concern for the poor and the oppressed went into Bart's soul. After college, he founded a missions organization called "Kingdom Builders Supply," which helps suburban youth groups do inner-city youth work.

Quite a pair, these two Campolos. They are both making a difference in their world. What is the main job of a dad, according to Tony?

"Making a kid believe in himself is one of the most important things that a father can do for his son."[4]

Bill Cosby
Occupation: Internationally Famous Comedian and Actor
Kids: Five, Now Grown

No, I didn't get an interview with Bill either. But reading his book *Fatherhood* is the next best thing.[5] Bill loves kids, there is no doubt about it, yet he loves having *grown* kids because they are no longer living at home. His book is jammed with humorous insight.

What was he up against as a dad? The way kids behave! One of his kids purposely tripped a sibling. Bill asked why he stuck out his leg. His son's reply?

"Dad, I didn't know my leg was going out. My leg, it does that a lot."

Bill editorializes for us fathers, "If you cannot function in a world where things like this are said, then you better forget about raising children and go for daffodils."[6]

What was one thing he found frustrating? Sibling rivalry nearly drove him mad. His kids were always fighting, arguing, clawing one another, or plotting against each other. Bill says, "No matter how calmly you try to referee, parenting will eventually produce bizarre behavior, and I'm not talking about the kids . . . *you* will find yourself strolling down the road to the funny farm. . . ."[7]

It wasn't all stress and struggle in the Cosby house, however. His son was having trouble in school and was becoming an expert at lying as well. I'll let you read the story in the book (pp. 91ff). The boy turned around, stopped lying, and started doing great in his studies. Realizing he had turned the corner with his son, Bill states, "There are many good moments in fathering, but few better than that."[8]

What's the main job of a dad?

". . . no matter how hopeless or copeless a father may be, his role is simply to be there, sharing all the chores with his wife. Let her *have* the babies; but after that, try to share every job around. . . ."[9]

James Davey
Occupation: Vice President, The Christian & Missionary Alliance
Kids: Two, Ages Twenty-two and Twenty-five

First a popular pastor, then a well-respected executive in a rapidly growing denomination, James is esteemed by many around the country and the world. A gifted preacher, he raised his son and daughter while trying to balance church ministry with denominational responsibilities.

What did this pastor/father feel he was against?

"I was up against the world's system . . . a system that is neutral at best and in some cases aggressively anti-God and biblical values."

Did he have some frustrations trying to be a good father?

"Time. I wish I had spent more time with each of them individually. It has really hit me: we get only one chance to parent when the kids are young or teenagers. When the opportunity is gone, it's gone forever.

"Also, the subject of discipline was frustrating at times. How do you tailor to the needs and personality of the child, being equitable and fair? I was not always sure I was. I tried to use the same discipline formula on two kids who were radically different."

Jim had a instant reply as to what helped him as a father.

"I had a great model in my own father. I often asked myself, *What would dad have done; how would he have handled this?* I'll never stop being grateful for the example he was to me."

Jim had an important success with his kids too.

"We never lost communication with the kids. We were able to create an environment where they could talk to us."

What is the job of a father?

"The main job of a father is to model what a Christian man is and how he ought to behave . . . the most profound learning is the result of imitation."

James Dobson
Occupation: Founder, Focus on the Family
Kids: Two, One College Age and One Career Age

We've seen a glimpse of the high-profile Tony Campolo as a father. How about the man who, in the minds of millions, represents the best and wisest there is when it comes to the Christian family today? Rolf Zettersten's biography of Dobson, *Turning Hearts Toward Home,* mainly concerns Dobson's ministry career, but it also gives us a few clues about his family life.

After Dobson's book *Dare to Discipline* rocketed him into national prominence, he was in high demand as a speaker. At first, he accepted those invitations. Then it hit him: How could he be a good father if he was never home? To the stunned horror of his agent, Dobson canceled all but two of his upcoming speaking engagements. [10] His ministry continued to enlarge through video, radio, and writing.

What kind of dad was Dobson? Letters received from his now grown children on a recent Father's Day give us a good idea:

From his daughter:

> Dear Dad,
> You are the best father that God ever created on this earth. I knew before all the fame and glory, at the ripe old

age of three, that I had a very special and unique Dad. The world found this out much later. Through the years, I have never doubted your love for me. I've always known that deep in that rusty heart of yours was the kind of love most children only dream of.

You are my father, my special friend . . . P.S. If I could change you, I wouldn't.

Danae

From his son:

Dad,

Well, as usual this is a last minute card, but it's not a last minute thought. Dad, I love you more than words can say. I never know how to express that idea right on paper, but I'm doing my best. I am going to miss you so much next year [first year away at college]. But I have one last thing to say, I will make you proud. I won't fail you, I promise.

Ryan[11]

Well, Dobson must have done at least a couple of things right as a dad.

Art Gerdes
Occupation: Oncologist
Kids: Three, Ages Twenty-four, Twenty-two, Sixteen

Art is known for a kind heart large enough to handle the hurt and desperation he sees every day as a cancer specialist. The Gerdes home has been "home base" for many hundreds of young people through the years as he and his wife have assisted in youth groups. Their large home and yard are filled with things that teenagers enjoy: pool table, Ping-Pong, volleyball, and hot tub.

I asked him what he felt he has been up against as a dad.

"It's time, no doubt. I work long, exhausting hours. Second, when I come home, I'm fatigued emotionally and physically. When I walk in the door, I don't want to hear about stress or problems. I want to hear about good things that will make me happy and bring me up. You can't imagine what it's like to work with cancer patients day in, day out.

"Another thing I'm up against is how different my upbringing was from how things are today. I was raised on a farm, by a *very* strict father and mother in a very strict Mennonite church. The law was the law was the law, and that was that. Disobedience never entered the realm of possibility. Well, my kids don't feel that way today, that's for sure. It's still hard to keep myself from reverting to a heavy-handed approach with them."

As to what helped him the most in his efforts to be a good father, Art paused and then smiled.

"It was seeing others who have gone through it before. I watched other men handle their kids. I learned a lot this way."

I asked him about successes, and his view of his main job.

"I've succeeded in instilling in each of them a sense of respect, consideration, and kindness toward people. They know the value of human life and personhood. My job as a dad has been to provide for my family and to be an adviser and teacher, a supporting and spiritual leader."

Dave Gowe
Occupation: Elementary School Teacher
Kids: Three, College Age, Career Age

Dave has been very active as a Christian layperson and professional Christian educator. He is highly regarded by his colleagues in the public schools as well as those in the church. What was he up against as a dad?

"My own spiritual weakness," was his immediate reply. "So many times I would react to my boys in the flesh, not the Spirit. Second, I felt I was up against the incredible pressure on them to be like the world.

"My greatest frustration was when John had his 'off years.' This was during much of high school. He was far from God, and the most frustrating thing for Bev and me was that we couldn't communicate with him. He shut us totally out of his life. Though he lived right here, we lost touch completely. This was very, very hard."

What about a success he felt?

"Number-one success, despite John's off years, was and still is our family dinner hour. From the very beginning, we made family dinner together a high priority. After the meal and the dishes were cleared, we would drink coffee or tea and just talk. If Bev and I were out of town or got extra busy, the boys reminded us to get our act together. Still today, our married son and his wife frequently come over and sit with the four of us after dinner. We love to just communicate."

And what does Dave feel his job was and is as a father?

Again, there was not a moment's hesitation.

"To model positive Christian living."

Ron Habermas
Occupation: Christian Education Professor
Kids: Three, Ages Thirteen, Nine, Five

Ron is a wonderful combination of humor, scholarship, and concern for others. He is well loved by his students and well respected by his peers. His foundations-to-practice book of Christian education, a research project six years in the making, is scheduled for release in 1992.

I asked him what roadblocks he feels keep him from being as good a father as he wants to be.

"I miss too many teachable moments. Sometimes I'm angry instead of sensitive. Sometimes I say the wrong thing. I've got to get better at these things."

How about a frustration?

"It's hard to be proactive instead of just reactive. I wish I could somehow spend more quality time with my girls, one-on-one. Each is so different from the other. I'm trying to improve, though. I'm taking my nine-year-old fishing on Saturday, and we're both excited."

I found Ron's reflection on a success he has felt especially insightful.

"I think I've done well at customizing my parenting to the three very different personalities of my daughters. It takes a lot of thought to be sensitive to their differences and individuality. I feel good about how things have gone so far."

Actually, there is something in his job that has helped him succeed as a father, something from which he is always learning.

"I work with students all day. That means every day I see how different they are from one another. As a professor, it's not good enough to treat them all the same, to just give out pat answers and standard formulas to their questions. Each one is special and unique. It's made me more sensitive to my own girls.

"My main job as a dad is to help my girls realize they can be partners with God, to help them find their special niche, and to encourage them in what God has called them to do."

Mike Yaconelli
Occupation: Pastor and Co-Founder, Youth Specialties
Ministries
Kids: Five, Ages Twenty-three, Twenty-one, Eighteen,
Sixteen, Thirteen

The organization Mike founded, Youth Specialties Ministries, is famous around the country for quality resources, youth
leader training events, and conventions. Mike is famous as a
passionate communicator. It is a passion to see young people
and their leaders be radically committed to the Gospel of Jesus
Christ. As a father what, for him, were obstacles to being a
good dad?

"For me it was, and still is, choosing the right issues to confront
with our kids. What is important and worth making an issue of,
and what is not? Here's an example: My kids are preacher's kids,
right? So, do I make church attendance mandatory on Sunday
morning? We decided no. If they are out late the night before or
are just too tired, they don't have to go. It's expected that they'll
normally go, but I give my kids the same latitude I give others in
the church when it comes to Sunday A.M. attendance.

"Another thing I constantly feel I'm up against as a father is
this: 100 percent of our culture contradicts what our values are as
Christians. What I do and hold true as a parent is cut down by
their friends, their school, TV, music, and movies. Sometimes
I've felt very lonely because of this."

I asked him what helped him the most in being a good dad,
and his answer was a real surprise.

"Mistakes. Mistakes helped me improve the most as a father.
My kids would call me on something, and I'd have to apologize
and ask their forgiveness. I think it's wrong when a parent doesn't
admit weakness and failure to a kid.

"Another thing that has helped me is a healthy view of time.

What I mean is what seems so all-important now probably won't seem so important later. This helps me not be so uptight about issues. One of my sons got bad grades in high school—Cs, Ds, maybe an occasional B. No matter what I said, no matter what my wife and I did, this didn't change. What happened when he went to college? Boom. Straight-A student. How do you figure that one?"

Mike feels good about being a dad and highlighted two successes he is happy about.

"This is going to blow your book, but I'll say it anyway. One success I've had is that we haven't forced Christianity on our kids. They're around Christianity all the time since they're PKs [preacher's kids], so we never had family devotions, prayer times, that sort of thing. Yet each one is pursuing a relationship with Christ. It's really great.

"Second success is humor. All my kids have a good sense of humor, and I feel I've been able to pass that along to them."

How about his view of the main job as a dad?

"Lead kids by earning the right to be heard. I love it now when my oldest boys give me a call and ask me for advice and we talk. I matter to them, and my advice is respected. I've worked hard at earning that respect."

We've looked over a lot of shoulders in the last three chapters. Now it's time to start applying. We've gotten the point that we are not alone in our efforts at fathering. Now let's move on, run some plays, get practical, and learn to be better fathers ourselves.

Questions for Discussion

1. Give your answers to the questions on page 79.

2. What is one Scripture that has helped you or given you encouragement as a father? Share that verse with your group.

Idea Corner 5

With Preschoolers

Feeling cabin fever when it's raining outside? Don't be sad, be happy . . . it's only on rainy days you can go puddle splashing with your son or daughter. Forget about staying dry. Just put on a hat, coat, and head for puddle jumping and splashing madness. A good hot bath and a nice bowl of soup make a fitting end to a puddle-jumping adventure.

With Elementary Age

Make an adventure out of learning a new culture. Pick a country, visit the local library, and come home with a travel book about your choice. After appropriate study, visit a restaurant that features food from that country.

With Teenagers

There is much emphasis in schools these days about being kind to the environment. Take a Saturday morning and do a litter patrol on your street. Go to a nearby park and do the same. Find a stream and make sure one hundred yards of it are litter-free on both banks. Call your city or county parks department for suggested projects and ideas. If there is U.S. Forest Service land not far from where you live, inquire about the "Adopt a Trail" program.

Part III

Our Jobs as Dads

6

Planned Fatherhood

My wife and I had a two-month-long honeymoon. A good friend had advised us to take as much of the summer off as possible and get our marriage started strong. After a foray south to Disneyland, we came back to western Washington for six weeks of camping and backpacking.

The Gothic Basin Trail in the north Cascades doesn't fool around. It's an old miners' trail that doesn't bother with frills and subtleties like switchbacks. *Trail* might be too kind a word. *Scramble* is more accurate. It just goes up—three thousand feet in two and a half miles. With heavy backpacks, it took us six hours to go the first two miles. Slowly, before our eyes, the flora changed from near rain forest to alpine. We showered in each welcome waterfall that splashed from the cliffs above as the hot afternoon sun made this hike memorable for less-than-pleasant reasons.

Finally, nearing the ridge crest, we rounded a bend and saw it: a steep, snow-filled gully stretched in front of us. We could see the trail emerge from the snowfield about seventy-five feet above and ahead of us. We could also see that, just beyond, the path leveled and entered the basin.

95

My heart sank as I surveyed the scene. Go around above? No chance. Snow and ice hugged a vertical cliff. Go around below? Looking down was enough to make even a mountain goat nervous. Trudge on over the steep and slippery snow? I didn't recall suicide being in our wedding vows.

What did we do? We quit, that's what we did. Five minutes in reverse found us a little ledge to prayerfully pitch our tent. Next morning we scrambled down, got in the car, and two hours later we happily unpacked in a nice, level state campground at the beach.

We had hit an obstacle that we couldn't or wouldn't cross. What keeps men from becoming better fathers? What obstacles turn us back from reaching new heights in fathering or keep us from starting up the trail in the first place? Once we've labeled the obstacles in our path, how do we learn to overcome them?

In the questionnaire below, rate yourself on a 1–5 scale. "1" is "This is completely untrue for me" and "5" is "Yes, this is totally true for me."

Obstacles to Better Fathering

_____ 1. My own father was a terrible example.

_____ 2. I wasn't raised to be caring or nurturing . . . this was never praised or encouraged.

_____ 3. Mothering seems to come so naturally to my wife, and she seems so good at it, I just naturally let her handle the kids.

_____ 4. Honestly, I don't much like the way my kids behave. It's really hard to even want to be involved with them.

_____ 5. I see my main role as that of breadwinner for the family. I let my wife do most of the parenting.

_____ 6. Frankly, I'm caught in a rat race, and though I
may want to be a better father, there's just no
time.

How many 4s or 5s did you score? These are the steep snowfield
barriers to flourishing fatherhood. Let's look at each issue. What's
the problem? How can we, by His grace, plan to make progress?

Issue #1: Doomed From Day One

Scriptural Base

". . . punishing the children for the sin of the fathers to the
third and fourth generation . . ." (Exodus 20:5).

"He just never had a chance."

Susan looked at me through her red and watery eyes. Taking
a deep breath, she continued.

"His dad was a cold, sullen, and angry man. He never, ever,
praised his kids. Bob was never shown how to do anything else.
That's what he's like now . . . he's just like his father. It kills me
to see what it's doing to Justin."

This sad scene is repeated hundreds of times a year across the
country in the offices of pastors and counselors. The names
change, but the cast of characters remains constant. Fearful,
sometimes victimized women, having suffered in silence for only
God knows how many years, finally seek help. They seek help
because they feel their own lives, their own personhood, being
systematically disassembled by a controlling and authority-
intoxicated male. They seek help because they see sadness and
hurt growing into fear and anger in their own children, especially
the sons.

At "best," a father who has grown up with a terrible father
is withdrawn, uncommunicative, and seemingly present in the
home only physically. At worst, the father is a raging hurricane

of angry demands or a volcano of abusive outbursts. I am reminded of fathers like this almost every day. Not far from church, I pass one of the secret safe houses in Seattle for women and their children who are fleeing domestic violence. I've seen fear-filled children tumble out of taxicabs clutching dirty teddy bears. I've seen bruised-cheeked mothers struggle to carry their trash-bagged belongings up the stairs to the security entrance.

An unhealthy pattern of fathering that took ten to eighteen years to learn is not likely to be reversed quickly. However, if you realize you are suffering from an unhealthy model father, you take a huge positive step by reading a book like this.

Are you already seeking to be more devoted to Christ and devoted to fathering (chapter 2)? Good. That's an essential beginning.

Forgiveness is the next step. First, you must look backward. It is crucial to mentally forgive your father for the mistakes he made. You must let go of your own bitterness, disappointment, and sense of injustice for what you experienced. The mental reprogramming may take months, but reprogram you must. When your mind tries to replay a painful incident, you must immediately run to the Lord in prayer and, instead of watching that mental tape, change channels immediately. Use every negative memory that pops on the screen as a trigger for praise and thanks to God. It's not the memory you praise God for. Look for something else worthy of praise and thanks— something about Him you enjoy, something positive about your spouse, kids, world. Praise changes hearts and minds.

Second, look upward on your forgiveness agenda as you seek forgiveness from God. The negative, unhelpful traits so aptly picked up are aptly inflicted on your family. Are you sullen, possessive, jealous, angry, controlling, or touchy? Sins, every one. None of these represent the fruit of the Holy Spirit. It takes courage to name sin as sin, and you must do it if you have any hope of getting beyond the steep snowfield that blocks the way.

Having looked backward and upward in forgiveness, now look forward to your wife and children. Admitting wrong and asking forgiveness are among the hardest things possible for a man to do. The very words *I was wrong* tend to get stuck in the voice box as pride frantically searches for another way to deal with the issue.

"I was wrong for _____, please forgive me," though hard to say, will build bridges and restore relationships. These words are capable of arresting the collapse of a marriage and the dissolution of a family.

The forgiveness process, though admittedly agonizing, begins to aim you in the right direction for the future. Depending on the seriousness of the negative parental hangover you experience, some sessions with a good Christian counselor can help further clarify the action steps necessary for positive change. A good written resource is *Unfinished Business: How a Man Can Make Peace With His Past* by Donald Joy (Victor Books, 1989).

Issue #2: Raised to Be a Macho Man

Scriptural Base

"But the wisdom that comes from heaven is first of all pure; then peace-loving, considerate, submissive, full of mercy and good fruit, impartial and sincere" (James 3:17).

"Get rid of all bitterness, rage and anger, brawling and slander, along with every form of malice. Be kind and compassionate to one another, forgiving each other, just as in Christ God forgave you" (Ephesians. 4:31, 32).

It can be a rough-and-tumble world for a boy who is trying to become a man. GI Joe, Rambo, and Transformer play eventually give way to hard-hitting football and intensely competitive wrestling. Were we strong enough, brave enough, daring enough with our bodies to gain the approval of our dads and our peers? A boy who is rewarded only for reckless and aggressive behavior as a ten-year-old may find it hard to hold a baby fifteen years later. A decade after this, he may feel equally uncomfortable when confronted with a sobbing daughter or a son who is interested in art, not sports.

Did we ever hear, "Don't be a sissy," or "That's the way girls are, don't be like that"? Some of us were rewarded by our fathers only for behavior that fit his paradigm of manhood.

I see the obvious outcome of this fathering pattern whenever I volunteer at the local elementary school. Some nine-year-old boys are "nice." They get along well with everyone, including girls. Other boys, however, are nearly unstoppable in their aggressive behavior. They practice karate, hurl verbal insults, and behave as if they would kill if they only had real machine guns. They assault one another first. When this becomes boring, they target the classroom furniture or the girls, between which they seem to make little distinction.

Some of us were never raised to be caring or sensitive. That was to be avoided at all costs. Real boys, real men, acted like it. Unfortunately, the macho man image may play well on TV commercials or in Hollywood movies, but it gets bad reviews at home. Double-shift, stressed-out mothers and self-esteem-assaulted children don't need a dad who is an archetypal Rambo.

Remember the final scenes in *Rambo: First Blood Part II*? Our "hero," frustrated by the feigned interest of the U.S. government in Vietnam MIAs, expresses his machismo in a definitely unsubtle way. At the end of the movie, he grabs a huge machine gun off its helicopter mountings, slings a few hundred bullets around his neck, and heads for the control center. He enters the center and empties a few hundred rounds into the computers and communications equipment that festoon the room. Bashing down

another door, he finds the quivering and sniveling U.S. government official. His twelve-inch hunting knife against the neck
helps underscore that Rambo is ticked off in a major way. His
point duly made, Rambo swivels around and walks off across a
grassy field, muscles bulging.

It works in the movies, but it doesn't work at home. Showing
little or no care and sensitivity at home is an excellent way to
lose both wife and family.

If you recognize that you were not raised or praised to be caring
and sensitive, what do you do? As with Issue #1, becoming
devoted to Christ and to family is the proper basis.

A next step is to find a mentor. A what? A mentor is someone
who teaches by his actions more than by his words. In this case,
a mentor is a Christian man who knows how to show care and
sensitivity at home. If you don't know how, you need to admit
your need and openly build a bridge.

"Say, Jack, you and I have known each other awhile, right?
Well, I notice you're pretty good with your kids. You seem to like
them and enjoy them. They feel the same about you. This is hard
for me to admit, but I've never really learned how to be much
more than Mr. Macho, and I can see it's not going over too well
at home. Could I get some time with you, regularly, so we can
talk about this stuff? And could our families get together once in
a while so I can see how you act around the home?"

It takes a real man to admit weakness. However, if you enter
into a mentoring relationship with someone who lives what you
need, you will learn about fathering.

Issue #3: Living With an Expert

Scriptural Base

"Fathers, do not exasperate your children; instead, bring them
up in the training and instruction of the Lord" (Ephesians 6:4).

Most women seem born to be good mothers, but some of these are *really born to be mothers*. They live to enjoy the children. There is nothing they would rather do than read to, play with, and enjoy those kids. They would be lousy attorneys, executives, or investment bankers, but wow, are they good mothers!

Living with an expert can be tough on one who isn't. Perhaps you would like to be involved with the kids more and be a better father, but there's no room. Your spouse monopolizes the kids and even scoffs at your feeble attempts at parenting. Scripture says, however, that fathers are to be involved in "bringing up" the kids.

Don't laugh. In one major study, 40 percent of the men surveyed wanted more involvement with their kids, but 70 percent of these reported their wives were definitely against it. The wives saw their husbands as incompetent fathers, and they didn't want the power dynamics in the home to be messed with.[1]

How does one learn to be a better father if he is either given no chance or is just too intimidated?

The first step . . . can you guess? If you are growing in devotion to the Lord and growing in devotion to the family, your spouse will notice the change in you. This can open the door to the second step, communication.

"Dear, you are such a good mother, I'm in awe of how great you are. I want to say that your being so good kind of scares me, and I feel pretty incompetent in comparison. Could you please help me get more involved with the kids? I really want to learn how."

In chapter 8, we'll see what special part a father plays in the unique development of sons and daughters. The woman cannot, studies have shown, do it all successfully. Looking at this research may open the eyes of an otherwise reluctant wife/mother.

Issue #4: Kids Who Aren't Very Likable

Scriptural Base

"Finally, brothers, whatever is true, whatever is noble, whatever is right, whatever is pure, whatever is lovely, whatever is admirable—if anything is excellent or praiseworthy—think about such things" (Philippians 4:8).

Some of us struggle with learning how to be better fathers because, quite honestly, we don't much care for our kids. Yes, we love them because we're supposed to, right? But *like* them, now that can be a real challenge.

Remember in chapter 2 we saw a few of the things there are to wonder at in each stage of a young person's growth. Well, there are things that turn us off too.

Newborns   They steal our sleep and vastly complicate our lives. We may feel abandoned by our wives as they focus so intensely on this new life that has come into the home.

Toddlers   Our prize possessions mean nothing to an eighteen-month-old. He or she will pull it down, chew on it, vomit on it, and who knows what else on it. Toddlers are *work*. They can't be left unattended where there is any chance of danger or harm.

Twos and Threes   If we had any doubts about an inherited sinful nature, these doubts are dispelled when Johnny hits two. He's old enough to know what he wants and smart enough to make the rest of his world mighty miserable until he gets it.

Fours and Fives   Now parenting is getting expensive. Clothes and toys cost more. Sally sees an ad for something on TV and she wants it. Kids, especially boys, who are accident-prone begin to blossom in their ability to break things and themselves at this age.

Six- to Ten-Year-Olds   These can drive a man stark raving mad. One expert puts it this way:

> . . . many fathers really expect [middle childhood] boys to be calm, decorous, prompt, courteous, unselfish, quick to do any chores assigned, clean, careful not to tear his clothing or get it dirty, always willing to listen to adult instructions, and always careful to keep his room clean and his clothes hung up. Middle childhood boys, and girls, are obviously NOT that way. The sooner a father accepts all their immature, childish qualities the easier it will be and the better the relationship he will have with his child.[2]

Eleven- to Thirteen-Year-Olds   At this age, kids can become monsters overnight. They are prone to display hormone-induced emotional ups and downs that are hard to predict and even harder to live with.

Fourteen- to Sixteen-Year-Olds   Middle adolescents can think they are much wiser than their parents and feel their status is severely reduced by being associated with parents at all. As fathers we may think, *After all these years of stress, this is the thanks I get.*

Seventeen- to Nineteen-Year-Olds   Young people this age have little use for parental advice, structure, or strictures. They are immortal, invincible, and won't be bothered with the sadly outmoded and outdated opinions we may have.

Looks pretty bad, doesn't it? How in the world do we learn to overcome these and other feelings if we're having them? If we are fathers in the Word, we're learning to have God's heart for Himself *and* our kids. To make more progress will take some effort, but it's worth it.

Go to the store and buy a notebook and pen. Put them some-place convenient. Every time you see something you don't like about your kid, march to the notebook and write down some-thing wonderful about the child or something you like about him or her. This may take considerable effort and creativity at first, depending on how unlikable the kid really is.

Your nine-year-old boy breaks a window? Write, "He's a strong kicker," or, "He doesn't swear at his mom."

Your sixteen-year-old girl treats you as if you have leprosy? Write, "She's not pregnant," or, "She's getting good grades in most of her classes."

Yes, this is work, no doubt about it. Yet Scripture tells us to think about the good. As we do, the Lord will begin to change the way we think. Do this for three weeks and see for yourself how it can change your attitude about a difficult son or daughter. Don't stop after three weeks!

This exercise can be taken a step further, of course, as you eventually share your positive comments with your son or daugh-ter. No, your nine-month-old won't much care that "at least she doesn't cost much to feed," but kids start benefiting from com-pliments not many months later. A father who sees the good in a son or daughter, despite the hassles and despite the bad stuff, will fortify a child's or young person's self-esteem.

Issue #5: Bringin' Home the Bacon

Scriptural Base

"Then the Lord said, '. . . For I have chosen him, so that he will direct his children and his household after him to keep the way of the Lord by doing what is right and just, so that the Lord will bring about for Abraham what he has promised him' " (Gen-esis 18:17–19).

Fathers, we are to be involved with our families. As God directed Abraham to be proactive in his family's life, the same is true today. Some might wonder why this even needs to be said. Yet the opposite attitude still exists among dads today, especially among those who work long, stress-filled hours. We may come home at the end of the day feeling as if all the life and energy has been sucked out of us. After a hassled ten hours dealing with disasters, absorbing criticism, and trying to be patient with worm-mentality associates, we just don't have anything left when we hit home.

John's got a schoolwork problem. "Mary, would you help your son with his homework?" Pam's hurting over unrequited love. "Pray about it dear, there are more fish in the sea, know what I mean?"

Dads who are only physically present may try to console themselves because they are "providing" for the family, but providing what?

If you are a bringing-home-the-bacon kind of father either by upbringing or by job choice, you must see this as a problem. Talk this through with your spouse or a close friend. What, specifically, can you do in the coming week to be more a participant in the home? What can you do and, having decided, when will you do it? All the ideas included at the end of the chapters are excellent for learning to be more involved in the home. But what if you want to and there's no time?

Issue #6: Going Nowhere, But Very Fast

Scriptural Base

"These commandments that I give you today are to be upon your hearts. Impress them on your children. Talk about them when you sit at home and when you walk along the road, when you lie down and when you get up" (Deuteronomy 6:6, 7).

We can call it many things: the rat race, the hurried pace, the overbooked/overscheduled life. Call it whatever, many men know what it is by experience. There isn't much time for the day-to-day teaching by word and example highlighted in this familiar passage from Deuteronomy.

Answering these questions will help us focus on the two main issues of the fast-track life and its effect on fathering.

My Work, My Time

1. I normally work at my job:
   - (a) less than 40 hours a week
   - (b) 40–50 hours a week
   - (c) 50–60 hours a week
   - (d) more than 60 hours a week
2. When I am at work, my job is intense, pressured, and stress-filled:
   - (a) hardly ever
   - (b) sometimes
   - (c) most of the time
3. When I am at home or otherwise "off," I think about my job:
   - (a) rarely
   - (b) occasionally
   - (c) much of the time
4. I have adequate time each day for a quality devotional life:
   - (a) rarely
   - (b) occasionally
   - (c) most days

5. I have adequate time each day to play with, talk with,
    or help my kids:
    (a) rarely
    (b) occasionally
    (c) most days
6. My kids feel:
    (a) I don't spend nearly enough time with them
    (b) I spend enough time with them occasionally
    (c) I am generally successful at spending enough
         time with them

My Work   In questions 1, 2, and 3 above, score a 1 for each
a, 2 for each *b,* and so on. Add your score. Write it here:____
Score:

Less than 6	No rat race evidenced here.
6–8	On the edge, caution needed.
More than 8	Improvement definitely needed.

If you scored anything above a 6, you need to take an honest
look at your employment and its effect on your life.

The effects of high-pressure and time-demanding jobs are blaz-
ingly clear. No man seems able to shield his family from the
spillover effects of this kind of work.[3] Upwardly mobile profes-
sionals and executives are among the least interested in spending
time with their kids or having non-work-related interests.[4] Some
parents feel they can have "quality time" with their kids, despite
their frenzied schedules. Unfortunately, "quality time" doesn't
often happen when parents come home exhausted and stressed.
Quality time isn't something easily programmed. It more naturally happens as a serendipitous subset of large, unpressured
amounts of time.[5]

Why do we work so much to the exclusion of our families?
Money. Time is money, right? It's hard to argue with because it's

so plainly true: more money equals less time with family, and more family time means less money.[6] Some of us have not only bowed to the mistress of materialism but have also taken up the dance with gusto. Or, as one writer put it, "Today's men . . . buy things they don't need with money they don't have to impress people they don't like."[7]

The financial pressure we heap upon our backs with credit-card debt can be mind-numbing. Recently, I intended to explore this idea further by spending an hour in the clerk's office of the Federal Bankruptcy Court in downtown Seattle. It was not a pleasant afternoon outing, and about forty minutes was all I could take. Bankruptcy files are a matter of public record, and heaped in front of me were *hundreds* of cases from only the last two months.

I sat down with an armload of cases and studied them page by unhappy page. K.N. had $42,486 in debts on thirteen charge accounts. After spending all that money, he had assets of only $5,308 to show. Mr. & Mrs. J. had $88,223 of debts piled on only ten credit card accounts. Imagine the burden of paying 15 to 20 percent interest on $88,000 of credit-card debt! Of the few dozen cases I scanned, the average person had five major credit cards and five department store cards. I'm sure it was a wonderful life, but not for long. I scanned the "Judgments" file too, which would be better titled, "The Party's Over." As I said, I couldn't stomach this for long.

The point is this: Our hunger for material status is sometimes the reason we feel so burdened to work so hard. Why work hard? To get the money to finance the dream of affluence, or at least the illusion thereof. Left unchecked, this hunger will consume us, leaving us with no time or energy for fatherhood. Affluence can be an addiction that destroys our own soul first and then our families.

How many men do you know who, near the end of their lives, wished they had worked more hours and spent less time raising their kids? Take out a piece of paper and write their names. Chances are, you could think for an hour and not come up with even one name to put on the page.

How do we learn to get out of the rat race? As we are growing in our devotion to Christ and our devotion to our kids, our grip will loosen, finger by reluctant finger, on the craving to prove our manliness via the material. Some men make a conscious choice to find a different job or career. The concept is called *downshifting,* and it results in a fast-track slowdown.[8] It may take them a few months or a couple of years to pay off consumer debts, but once they do they may have the freedom to work less.

Another way we help ourselves is to make choices to settle for less. A friend recently spent eighteen thousand dollars on remodeling his kitchen. It is incredibly beautiful. Our kitchen, by comparison, is a joke. It's a 1940s make-over of a 1910 kitchen. Counter space is sparse. The floor looks as if someone used it for target practice. The cupboard doors don't close right. It is ugly, and my wife and I have used that kitchen "as is" since we moved in five years ago. We had in mind a major remodeling, but since we are growing in our devotion to Christ and in our commitment to our family, we decided we didn't need the financial and time pressure a total make-over would take.

Our scaled-down dream kitchen is going to cost us about fifteen hundred dollars. No marble countertops. No tile floor. I'll try to get the cupboard doors to close right. A carpenter will widen our counters and build us some shelves. We'll patch and paint. The finished product will never qualify for *Better Homes & Gardens* or *Good Housekeeping.* But who will ever be able to measure the benefit of saving ourselves from the financial and time pressure? Our children probably won't point to the kitchen decision as being *the* thing that saved them from a life of drugs and prostitution. But who knows . . . maybe they will. Ask me in a decade.

What if we simply and honestly can't work less? Then the issue becomes what we do with the leisure time we do have.

My Time   On the "My Work, My Time" questionnaire, look at questions 4 through 6. For every *a* score 3, *b* score 2, and *c* score 1. Improvement is a code red emergency if you score above a 6.

The use of leisure time is another subject interesting to people who make their living by studying people. In 1985, the average man in the United States worked 43.8 hours a week and had 41.1 hours of leisure a week, distributed as follows:

Hours Per Week

15.7	TV
5.0	visiting
3.5	talking
3.4	driving
2.9	sports/outdoor recreation
2.7	reading
2.2	adult education
1.9	outdoor yard work, etc.
1.2	thinking
.8	cultural
.8	clubs
.6	religion
.4	music listening[9]

We can learn to be better fathers as we learn to redirect some of our leisure time toward our children. I try to take individual time with each of my three daughters at least once each week. It is seldom convenient but always enjoyable. Where do I find the time? Our poor TV gets lonely, as I attend to it only two or three hours each week (except during football season, when I watch it four or five hours).

Each of us has our own schedules and priorities . . . no one suggestion is equally applicable to all. Yet an honest accounting of where our off time goes will probably turn up some chunks that can be redirected toward fathering.

It all takes planning, thought, and purpose. Once we have begun to make progress, however, how do we direct our efforts for the best results? Most of us want to see our kids grow up to be growing Christians, responsible, happy, and successful. How do we pass this torch to them?

Questions for Discussion

1. Share how you scored each of the six issues on the "Obstacles to Better Fathering" questionnaire.

2. Share your score on the "My Work, My Time" questionnaire.

3. What impacts, positive and negative, does your work have on your family?

4. Are you currently feeling financial pressure? In what ways, and how is this affecting your ability to be a good father?

5. Does any of your leisure time need to be redirected for a better walk with God or to be a better husband/father? What is one thing you can change?

6.   The author suggests a scriptural base for each of the six
        issues he presents in this chapter. Review these verses
        now. Which speaks the most to you right now?

Idea Corner 6

With Preschoolers

Children love to watch an electric train. So may the family cat
or dog. A basic HO scale set will cost less than thirty dollars, and
it is well worth the hours of fun. Add some building blocks,
LEGO bricks, and Fisher-Price people, and you've got the making of a megalopolis. When your son or daughter is old enough
to handle the major responsibility of running the controls, celebrate this stepping-stone of maturity.

With Elementary Age

Here is an unforgettable experience: Have a pudding fight.
Make the pudding with water, not milk. About a gallon for each
participant is about right. Caution: Do not have pudding fights
indoors, unless you can hose down your home without harm to
its contents. Have a hose nearby, because some people find pudding in the eyes can sting. Have camera or camcorder handy.
Invite your neighbors to join in or at least watch. You'll be
famous in the neighborhood!

With Teenagers

Are you anticipating the purchase of a "big ticket" item in the
coming twelve months? Is it something of interest to your teenagers, like a new car, boat, hot tub, or home remodeling? If so,

solicit their help in the decision-making process. For example, if you are thinking about a new car, have them help get opinions from others who have the same car and do research in *Consumer Reports.* Visit various car dealerships together. Become educated on negotiating skills. When you have picked the car, wheel and deal together with the salesperson. When the big purchase is finally made, make it no secret to your friends and relatives what a major help your son or daughter was in making this big decision.

Passing the Torch

Remember the front-page famous father named Eli in chapter 3? Somehow, he royally succeeded in fouling up the handoff of his faith and values to his young sons Hophni and Phinehas. As we have already seen, many fathers of the Bible managed to fail spectacularly in passing on faith and values to their sons.

The problem is still with us. Fathers abound who fail to pass the torch of faith, responsibility, and self-esteem.

Ralph is the chairman of the elders of his church. He and his wife have been vital Christians throughout their four children's formative and teen years. Yet as Ralph and his wife sit alone at their kitchen table, they can't help but wonder why all four of their sons have abandoned faith in Christ. Each one of them ceased any semblance of a Christian life a soon as they graduated from high school.

Warren is a successful pastor. People have grown in the Lord and new believers have been added to each of the two churches he has served in the last twenty years. He has been careful not to let church consume his life and has tried to be a good father. His son and daughter have both graduated from college. The son now lives with his non-Christian girlfriend. The daughter has decided to "find herself" and is heavily into the New Age movement.

There is an immense amount of pain in these stories. We may already see our kids slipping away from us and their faith in God, and we hope to reverse the trend. Or, we may want to do all we can before any danger signals appear. In either case, the wondering, the praying, and the concern is deeply felt in our hearts.

Handing Off a Vital Faith

Here are two sobering questions: If everyone in your church had a faith that was just as vital and dynamic as yours, what kind of church would it be in terms of spiritual aliveness? If your kids developed a faith exactly as strong as yours, how happy would you be?

It can't be more obvious. If we are going to hand off a vital Christian faith to our sons and daughters, we've got to have one in the first place. We've given this much emphasis already—being truly devoted to the Lord, with the same enthusiasm and devotion most of us so easily give to sports. Assuming we are all on the same team in this regard, sincerely wanting to grow in our devotion to *our* Father, what are some factors that should receive our focus? How can we pass the torch of faith to our children? Let's talk about attitudes first, then information.

Attitudes

Coaches preach it to their players. Instructors teach it to their students: "If you're going to win, if you're going to do well, attitude is everything." It doesn't hurt for us to view this faith-passing task as competition, because that is exactly what it is. It is spiritual warfare, as Paul says, "For our struggle is not against flesh and blood, but against the rulers, against the authorities, against the powers of this dark world and against the spiritual forces of evil in the heavenly realms" (Ephesians 6:12).

The prize in this warfare is none other than the hearts, souls, and minds of our kids.

So what attitudes will help us win this spiritual warfare? Before answering, here is one more mental exercise: If you were in a church as a child or teenager, take a piece of paper and write down everything you *specifically* remember learning. If you are normal, you'll recall a couple of things, but otherwise your paper will be blank. Now, take out a second piece of paper and write down what you remember about your Sunday-school teachers or your youth leaders. Again, if you are normal, this could take a long, long time. People taught you good curriculum, but you don't remember so much of what they taught as what you remember about them. If they were positive people who cared and shared with a smile, you remember them well. If your memory of them is good, no doubt you believed what they told you and tried to model the good in them.

They taught us good curriculum, but we studied them instead. Here are five winning attitudes that make for a young person's wanting and being willing to receive the faith of the father. Here they are:

Joy   Like a bases-loaded homer in the bottom of the ninth, joy brings the hearts of others to attention. It is to be one of the premier characteristics of the Christian. Paul reminds us, "Rejoice in the Lord! It is no trouble for me to write the same things to you again . . ." (Philippians 3:1).

Tense, high-volume, stress-filled words aimed at our kids make them reject, not respect, us and our teaching. Joy, by contrast, serves as an invitation to listen, pay attention, and learn more.

Gratitude   I was lying on the couch in an after-supper semi-sleep while the TV news droned on. I opened my eyes just enough to see my two-year-old daughter, with her back to me, at the fireplace. She was very busy making something "pretend." She turned with a huge smile on her face and, holding her two hands open together, she carefully walked in my direction. I raised up on one elbow and looked into those brimming but empty hands. Whatever it was she had concocted at the fireplace was now obviously being offered to me. I opened my hands, she gently placed the nothing into them, all without a word. I thanked her again and again. With each thank-you, her face grew brighter and her shoulders grew straighter with pride.

I don't know if sincere gratitude plays well on Broadway, but I do know it plays well in Peoria. A home where a father shows gratitude for the slightest consideration, the tiniest kindness, even from a child, is a home where the child is learning to live like and be like the dad.

We can learn to be more thankful if we daily look for the little things our kids do right. If we have trouble finding something they do right, we can at least praise what they don't do wrong. "Gosh, Mary, thanks for not swearing at your mom tonight during dinner . . . I really appreciate it when you consider other people's feelings."

Who needs gratitude? Why should we have to be so kind and sensitive? Ask yourself this: If you had your choice between a kind, gracious, and grateful boss and a grump, which would you choose? If your church were looking for a new senior pastor, would you rather have a gracious and grateful one or a macho snob? Whom would you rather work for; whom would you rather follow?

Would our kids characterize us as grateful or grumpy? If it is the latter, we can be sure we are gradually shutting off their respect for us. This respect shutdown will result in their being extremely susceptible to peer pressure when they enter their teen years.

Enthusiasm   Ask an eighteen-year-old to tell you about her favorite high school teacher. Chances are, that favorite teacher will be one who is filled with life and enthusiasm. Kids have energy. In childhood or the teen years, their bodies are bursting with seemingly limitless supplies of raw energy. Kids relate well to enthusiasm. Just about any task, even the mundane, can be made more fun if done with gusto mixed with a little humor.

It was a hot summer vacation afternoon. We had driven many hours to get to this lake for camping. We got to the campground, and all that remained unoccupied was a dusty plot of grass ringed by an even dustier dirt road. It was too late in the day for any Plan B, and I could sense the Kageler spirits sinking fast. Though I wanted to complain and feel miserable, mentally I prayed a quick prayer and said, "Well, home sweet home, here we are. You guys get some fruit out of the cooler and go sit over in the shade. I'll start to set up, and I'll call you when I need help. Just relax."

With a burst of energy, I started to sing about how hot and terrible the place was as I raced around setting up camp. My enthusiasm and humor seeped over to my family, and eventually they got with the program. As the sun set, and as the mosquitoes (having feasted on us for the last two hours) receded from the air, we decided that maybe the place wasn't so bad after all.

Wonder   Before leaving University Presbyterian Church in Seattle to serve at the Crystal Cathedral, Bruce Larson spoke at a gathering of pastors at our church. It was my job to welcome him and show him around. He wanted to see my office and the rest of the church facility. Though our church was very small compared with his, he made me feel he was interested in every last detail I could tell him. Everything was so wonderful to him. When it was time to listen to his talk, he had my attention. He had shown me wonder, and it made me like and respect him.

We have already discussed the wonderful things about each age period our children go through. Are you having a hard time getting a focus on just what wonder is? Call it sincere excitement about the world around us and the awesomeness of God's creation. We can show sincere excitement for the achievements and accomplishments of our children and teenagers.

To show sincere excitement about our kids, we need to first carve out the mental space to notice them. Many Christian men, as they commute home, come to an imaginary line they have drawn halfway between work and home. When they cross that line, they consciously leave the workplace behind. They begin thinking of and praying for their wife and kids. When they get home, they are not only present physically but mentally also.

Kindness   A friend of mine is the Christian Education pastor of a large church. He has a unique, ongoing problem. There is a man in his church who stands against about half of everything Kevin proposes. He crusades for his own ideas, which may or may not actually be workable. This guy is an ecclesiastical nuisance to Kevin and has been for years.

What makes the situation interesting is this aggravating man is also very kind. About once a year, he and his wife take Kevin and his wife to dinner at a nice restaurant. Every Christmas, there is a gift for Kevin, his wife, and each of his four kids. This man shows up unannounced at the church office, knocks on Kevin's door, and plops a care package on his desk. With a huge and sincere smile, he leaves without saying more than a sentence. No politicking, no hassle, just kindness. The result? Kevin likes this guy and does his best not only to listen to him but also to give his weird ideas a try, if at all possible.

Sincere kindness gets noticed by our kids. Even a sixteen-year-old "grunt stage" boy will notice when his dad gets out the

Armor All and shines up the tires on the son's car. Kindness makes our kids want to respect us and our values.

Passing on our faith is first of all an attitude issue. Joy, gratitude, enthusiasm, wonder, and kindness set the stage for our children to be open to our input. While there is no surefire guarantee of success, these attitudes powerfully communicate a loving Heavenly Father who cares for His kids. Even secular research shows that supportive and nurturant behavior on the part of the father greatly increases the acceptance of the values by the young person.[1]

Information

Passing on the faith is more than attitude, however. We must give some information, and we must have some too.

Salvation   This is the greatest gift we can give our kids. What an awesome joy to lead our own sons and daughters to Christ. To do so requires no degree in theology, no graduate work in seminary. As each of my kids got close to turning six, I had the fun of sitting down with them and going over the Gospel basics. We talked about God's love, our sin, Jesus' death on the cross, and what we must do to receive Him into our lives. Each of them prayed to receive Christ into her heart, and the event was duly recorded in her Bible.

Some men default on this privilege. They trust a Sunday-school teacher or youth leader to lead their children to Christ. If your kids are still young, and if you've been a loving father, you will find your kids eager to respond to your leading them into salvation.

The Other Side   A second category of information to pass along that makes for a vital faith seems like a paradox, but it is crucial. Never let them forget what they have been saved from. *We need to teach them what the "other side" believes and why.* My wife and I began to talk about non-Christians with our kids even before kindergarten. We've talked about other religions, cults, alcoholism, drugs, why it makes sense to believe the Bible, and much, much more. We've taken field trips too.

When my three kids were in first, second, and fourth grade, we took them to a heavy metal rock concert. As our ears ached, we picked our way through the elaborately coiffured and heavily leathered-and-chained concertgoers dancing in the aisles. Finally, we got up close enough to the stage to really see how hellish the whole scene was. Our ears and eyes could take this assault less than a half an hour. The result? The three Kageler girls have a passionate hatred of heavy metal music and the life-style it encompasses. No, they are not all grown and out the door yet, but I'm 99.9 percent sure they'll never turn in that direction for identity or solace.

It's fun to teach kids to reject the sin but love the sinner. We really emphasize the distinction and that God loves sinners as much as He loves us, because we're sinners too. Several years ago, we sold our home in the safe suburbs of Seattle and moved into the infamous University District of the city. It's a great place to live and has a lot of conveniences. For faith development, it's a great place to live too. Punk rockers, drunkards, and panhandlers are commonplace. We are often reminded what we are saved from.

When we first moved in, my wife was taking the kids for a walk on the "Ave." Passing a group of spike-headed punkers, our youngest, then age five, said, "Mommy, why do they look so awful?" Janet wisely said, "Everyone wants to feel special, Hilary, and those kids just don't know yet that it is Jesus who can make them feel most special of all."

The public schools have been excellent for faith development. My daughters' faith has received much affirmation, as there are many Christians who are teachers in Seattle schools. On the other hand, each of them has been mocked for her faith, and they have learned firsthand that Jesus' words are true: "Blessed are you when people insult you, persecute you and falsely say all kinds of evil against you because of me. Rejoice and be glad, because great is your reward in heaven, for in the same way they persecuted the prophets who were before you" (Matthew 5:11, 12).

Many times, we have prayed together as a family for God to speak through us to our friends and neighbors. It is really exciting to see answers to these prayers. Living in this environment has made all five of us more missionary-minded.

We've got a visit to a New Age bookstore coming up soon. My kids are old enough now to recognize New Age teaching and its paraphernalia.

My goal as a father in all of this "other side" exposure and teaching is simple. When my daughters graduate and move on to college, they'll soon sit in their first sociology, anthropology, or philosophy class. If a professor portrays Christianity as an out-moded and unmodern religious hangover, I don't think my kids will be shocked. They'll have seen and heard it all before. If they get to know that professor, maybe they'll have a chance to run their fingers along the edge of his or her soul. When they come to the inevitable crack, they'll know how to apply the Gospel.

Far beyond teaching correct information and arming kids to live in the real world, we fathers need to portray that we believe in a God who is actually alive and still active today. Our kids must see us seeking Him and thanking Him when our prayers are answered. Can I, as a father, point to anything in my life that has happened in the last week or two and can be explained *only* by the power of God? If the answer is yes, my kids will find it easy to call this God their own, because they will have seen again and again how God works in the lives of people.

There is one more category of information that is helpful when it comes to passing the torch of faith. Why do teenagers turn away from the church and God?

Dr. Robert Laurent interviewed over four hundred randomly selected high school students. In his book, *Keeping Your Teen in Touch With God,* Dr. Laurent presents ten reasons teens reject religion, and it is important for fathers to have these things in mind as kids enter the teen years. When you see a problem area beginning to develop, you can address it early before it becomes a major issue. Here are the ten reasons, in the order of their reported significance:

Causes for Teenage Rejection of Religion

1. Lack of opportunity for church involvement.
2. Negative media influence (TV, rock music, movies).
3. Poor relationship with parents.
4. Low self-esteem.
5. Poor relationship with youth pastor.
6. Negative peer influence.
7. Authoritarianism in parents.
8. Struggle for emancipation from parents.
9. Negative concept of religion.
10. Lack of family harmony.[2]

Many of these ten we've just discussed. Now let's look more closely at passing the torch of self-esteem and the torch of responsibility.

A Self-Esteem Sampler

Our society worships at the altars of great looks, great intelligence, and great wealth. Our sons and daughters, especially if they are teenagers, can barely get up in the morning without being reminded that they are deficient in one, two, or all three of these areas.

It's 6:00 A.M. and Mary's clock radio comes on softly. She lies there, and as the fog clears in her brain, she begins to hear one of the hundred or so radio and TV commercials she will absorb today.

". . . weight loss clinic . . . lose weight, look great, feel good about yourself. You'll lose pounds of fat in a few short weeks. . . ."

All day long our teenagers hear an outer voice telling them they need to look better, be cooler, or have a more upscale image to be happy and accepted.

In addition to the input they will receive through radio, TV, or magazine advertising, they may also have to go through the torture of put-downs throughout the day at school.

No matter how good-looking, smart, or monied our kids might be, there will always be someone compared with whom they will feel inferior.[3]

Feeling inferior will have consequences for our son or daughter. Author Ronald Hutchcraft suggests the following five consequences:

1. *Low self-esteem results in go-with-the-flow Christians.* The young person who feels insecure is not likely to stand against the negative peer pressure of friends. Their "friendship" will be seen as too important to risk losing over the trivial matter of Christian standards and morality.

2. *Low self-esteem makes a young person feel rejected.* A person acts weak, rejected, and is further put down by peers. It is a vicious circle that is hard to stop.

3. *Low self-esteem makes a young person an emotional cripple.* The one with a poor-self-image may spend a great amount of time wondering what people think of him or her. If we as adults or teenagers focus so much on ourselves that we cannot genu-

inely love or care about those around us, we proceed in life in only a halting and subnormal way.

4. Low self-esteem means the chance of wasted potential is very high. Pastor Noren looks eye-to-eye with eighth-grade son Jeremy, an awkward and clumsy boy with a contagious smile.

"You know, Jeremy, you are going to be the finest Christian young man this church has ever produced. God has great things in store for you!"

"He does?" Jeremy can't believe what he is hearing, but those words come back to him many times in the coming months and years. Sure enough, he begins to live up to the words of his astute pastor. Without that encouragement, Jeremy might have remained uncomfortable and unsure.

5. Low self-esteem can make a young person a moral pushover. The girl or guy who feels inferior will probably fall for the first prince or princess who comes along. If continuing the relationship means moral compromise, why not? "[S]He makes me feel so special. I just can't say no."[4]

How many of the ten characteristics listed below do you now see in your teen or preteen?

_____ 1. The campus clown.
_____ 2. Denying reality.
_____ 3. Withdrawal from peers.
_____ 4. Conforming without resistance.
_____ 5. Fighting the world.
_____ 6. Wishy-washiness in decision making.
_____ 7. Acting rejected.
_____ 8. Focusing only on self.
_____ 9. Missing potential.
_____ 10. Moral pushover.

A problem in any one of these areas may indicate inadequate self-esteem. Also, a problem in any one of these areas makes the young person vulnerable to peer pressure. We need not just sit idly by, however. We can help our sons and daughters!

James Dobson, in his best-seller *Hide or Seek* suggests several specific ways we can build our kids' self-esteem.

1. *We must examine our own values and how they are portrayed in our own homes.* Unfortunately, it is not unusual for fathers to worship at the altar of looks, brains, and money. Are we always commenting on the "good looks" of people we see on TV, in magazines, or at the mall? Have we also revealed our true values by showing our kids over and over that it is the "looking good" kids who will receive our attention? What kind of people do we, as fathers, like to be around? How important is appearance in our decision making? Similarly, are we praising our smart daughter while putting down our not-so-smart son?

When it comes to money, do we convey in our supper conversation and elsewhere that we won't be happy until we have as much as the Jones family? Our kids will pick up our values and internalize them well. If they sense that we are disappointed in how they look or think, we do devastating damage to their self-esteem.

If, honestly, we are disappointed by their looks and physical or mental abilities, we as dads will need to confess our attitudes to God and seek a more biblically based self-esteem for ourselves and our teenagers. Where, in Scripture, are we to find this biblical basis?

Have a Bible handy and look up these verses. Don't just settle for the summaries given, but read from the Source how we are to think about ourselves.

- Genesis 1:26–28   We are made in God's image.
- Psalm 139:1–6   God thinks we are so important that He knows all about us. . . . He cares so much for His creation.
- Psalm 139: 13–18   God is active in determining how we look. . . . He has a part in how things come together before we are born.
- John 3:16   God loved us so much that He made the ultimate sacrifice to get our attention and to have fellowship with us.
- Matthew 10:29–31   We are important to God.
- Ephesians 2:10   God is not finished with us yet . . . we *are* (not *were*) His workmanship.

It is certainly possible for us as fathers to have an improperly based self-image ourselves. Before we help our kids, we may need to help us. As we ponder these Scriptures and even check cross-references, we will see how valuable we are to God. We will understand that we are the Lord's sons and daughters. We are cared for by the King! Our Father happens to own the universe! One has to be comatose to not feel good about that.

2. Offer unconditional love and support. No matter how our kids look or what their potential physically or mentally, they need and deserve our support. God gave them to us and it is our job to be His vehicle of unconditional agape love toward them.

3. We must teach our kids and ourselves a no-knock policy. We should agree as a family not to put down ourselves or one another. What are some of these put-downs?

"I'm so stupid [ugly, clumsy, etc.]."

"I can't do anything right."

"I'll never be as good as. . . ."

They develop a tendency to think of themselves in this way because of the many outer voices they hear that we have already described.

For every self put-down we hear, we need to encourage an affirmation instead. Don't, however, jump in and demand an affirmation. First acknowledge the feeling expressed by the self put-down. For example, if we hear, "I can't do anything," we can respond, "Sounds like you're frustrated. Tell me about it." After listening and clarifying the underlying issues, we can then encourage them to name, out loud, three things they can do well. We can help them if they can't think of three.

4. *We must praise and affirm our kids daily.* Affirmation should become as natural to us as breathing. What if we honestly don't see a lot of behavior worth praising? Catch the kids not doing something bad, and praise them for that!

"Stacey, I really appreciate how you didn't yell at me when I asked you to clean up your room."

5. *We must help kids compensate.* This is one of the single most-helpful suggestions fathers can receive to assist the development of a positive self-image. If our young person feels he or she is not good at something, help him be good at something else!

Of course we want to raise our kids with the conviction that they are important, valuable, and worthy not because of what they do but because of who and Whose they are. Unfortunately, for some kids, particularly during the junior high years, this solid psychology and theology won't help much.

As the junior high years approach, we should consider how we can help our sons and daughters feel they are good at something. It should be something they can do—something tangible such as being a good skier, piano player, photographer, chess player, or whatever. It should be something young people can enjoy. Later, as they mature mentally, they will be more able to feel good about themselves because of who and Whose they are as opposed to what they can do.

6. *Keep a close eye on the classroom.* Because success in our society is so closely tied to being successful at school first, we must have an interest in how our kids are doing in school. Some of their self-esteem, or lack of it, will result from how they feel they are doing.

7. *Prepare for adolescence.* If we still have preadolescents in the home, we can help them prepare by giving them a specialty that will help their self-esteem later. Also, we can discuss with them some of the attacks they can expect on their own feelings about themselves. In short, we can help them understand what is coming for them, physically, emotionally, and socially.[5] The finest resource available is James Dobson's *Preparing for Adolescence* (Vision House, 1979). It comes as a book, a series of tapes, and a student workbook. Some parents take their son or daughter away for a weekend to listen to the tapes and interact with the material.

These are all practical things we can do as fathers to help our kids have a good self-image.

Passing On a Sense of Responsibility

What is responsibility? Simply put, it is our ability to react properly when the need arises.

To learn responsibility, a young person must first have a good role model. We as fathers, of course, are in the ideal place to model responsible behavior. Unfortunately, the opposite is also true: we can model irresponsible behavior too. Can we resist running up credit-card debt that finally reaches the point which brings financial disaster to our family? Can we resist gluttony, or will there be excuses instead of fitness? Can we resist alcohol and getting drunk? Are we able to avoid the trap of wasting family resources on the hope of winning the lottery?

Second, our sons and daughters must be given specific tasks around the home that are theirs and theirs alone to do. Making their own lunch, preparing the evening meal, taking out the garbage regularly, and feeding the pets are all examples of jobs around the house or apartment that need to be done by someone. If we give our kids real responsibility, we must not shelter them from the real consequences of their failure.

Of course, there must always be room for grace. However, if young people see that it really doesn't matter if they don't follow through on their jobs, we teach them irresponsibility. Our young people need not be sheltered from the fact that life is work . . . it is not all fun and games. On the other hand, if we give our kids work to do, we must also make sure there is time for fun and craziness too.[6]

Third, as our kids get older and demonstrate progress, we must gradually hand over to them areas of decision making that primarily affect them, not us. Buying their own clothes, deciding how to spend their own money, what TV programs they watch are all examples of small sectors of life that are controlled by us as parents but must eventually be handed over.

In Luke 15, we have the ultimate example of a parent handing over responsibility to his son. The prodigal son took his cash and happily went his own way. We aren't told whether his father had confidence he would do well or feared he would not be able to handle the freedom. Chances are, since patriarch authority and control over the family was so complete in biblical times, the son wasn't ready to handle his own checking account.

If the father had misgivings about his son's ability, we can still take note that the father didn't bail him out when he was in trouble. It is probable that the father, as well as the rest of the household, would have known of the fortunes or misfortunes of the son who took off. The father didn't send him more money or additional aid. He let the son experience the full consequences of his own actions. The father did love him, though, and was happy to graciously receive him back when he had learned his lessons.

We don't know if Jesus' parable was based on an actual incident He had become aware of. Did the son move out with the goal of living on the wild side? Perhaps he did not but succumbed to peer pressure. If he did not learn much responsibility at home, he was a sitting duck in a distant land. Out there in the real world, he learned that decisions have consequences—and when daddy wasn't there to pay the rent, he had to move in with the pigs.

Giving our kids real responsibility will occasionally result in disappointment, but even mistakes can be turned into times of learning.

We have looked at passing the torches of faith, self-esteem, and responsibility. Let's focus in even closer, now, and look for answers to special needs and opportunities we face as fathers.

Questions for Discussion

1. If everyone in the church you attend had a faith as dynamic and vital as yours, what would the church be like? Honestly, how pleased would you be if your kids developed a Christian life as good as yours?

2. Of the five winning attitudes (joy, gratitude, enthusiasm,

wonder, and kindness), which is most and which is least evident in your life right now?

3.   What is one act of kindness you can do for each of your kids in the coming week?

4.   Did you have a rebellion against religion at any time during your teen years? If so, which of the ten reasons listed applied to you? Which might apply to your own son or daughter?

5.   What responsibilities around the house did you have when you were in junior high school?

6.   Which of the Scripture passages on page 128 is most encouraging to you and why?

Idea Corner 7

With Preschoolers

Kids will be as litter-conscious as parents. Go on a neighborhood litter patrol with your son or daughter and finish off with an ice-cream cone as a reward.

With Elementary Age

Do your kids know what you do for a living? Can they picture you at work when they pray for you there? Take them with you to visit your workplace. Introduce them to your co-workers. Take them on a tour of the office or the whole facility. If possible, take them to lunch where you usually eat.

With Teenagers

Think back to your own teenage years. What were some of the most embarrassing things that happened to you? Be vulnerable . . . let your teenagers see the stress you faced and how you handled these things. Ask your sons and daughters if they have been embarrassed recently. By what? How did they handle it?

8

Special Considerations 1

Father-Daughter, Father-Son
How to Care When We Can't
Be There

Fathers and Daughters

"Dear Dad,

"I wonder if you have noticed the changes in your little girl, and I wonder if they bother you? I know they bother me. I see your daughter six hours out of every day, one spent in my class and the other five in the hallways of our junior high school. When she entered my class two years ago, she was bright, sparkling, and competitive. Today, as a ninth-grader, the vital and lively girl I knew has disappeared to be replaced by a shy, submissive, subdued teenager who wears tight jeans and too much makeup. She seems to have lost interest in her grade-point average and deliberately pretends not to know the answers to questions raised in class. She is hiding her light behind two shades of eye shadow and values her body more than her mind.

"Before you become too alarmed, let me tell you that she is not alone. As is typical with teenagers, she is one of a pack. Many of her equally bright and once active girlfriends suffer from the same disorder. I wish I could reassure you that this is only a passing phase that stops when puberty ends. Unfortunately, my years of experience and the current research on your daughter and others like her indicate the opposite. This is the time at which she is likely to go permanently underground with her abilities and never resurface to realize her potential.

"I know you love her very much. I know you want what is best for her. You care. . . . Rest assured, you CAN make a difference, for you hold the keys in your hands. More than you realize, you can have an impact on her life. You can equip her with the self-esteem and psychological health necessary to achieve her potential, and you can do it in spite of the obstacles of peer pressure and societal expectations to which she has been exposed.

"Your importance as the man in her life cannot be underestimated. Consider this: research studies on female achievers consistently show that a father's role is critical to his daughter's development. . . . Fathers who act as mentors to their daughters have a profound influence. By being the first supportive male in your daughter's life, you will be giving her the edge; the . . . confidence mandatory for the rigors of personal and professional achievement and a lasting foundation on which to build her life."[1]

I have seen the same sad pattern that prompted the author of this letter, Nicky Marone, to write his book. Happy, wonderful girls go into the tunnel of adolescence and come out unrecognizable for the worse. We, as dads, must realize the power we hold in our hands when it comes to how our daughters cope with, and adjust to, their unfolding femininity and future.

Actions and Attitudes

By age three, a little girl knows she's a girl and is different from a boy.[2] No father consciously sets out to ruin his daughter's life, but our actions and attitudes sometimes set up our daughters to fail. Here are some recipes for messed-up girls. Unfortunately, many fathers provide all the "right" ingredients to produce these walking wounded.

Young and Sexy

RECIPE: Take one authoritarian father who never or seldom shows love and acceptance of his daughter. Withhold verbal and physical affection at an early age. Show no interest in or approval of the daughter's strengths and abilities. Criticize frequently.
RESULT: An adolescent girl who is insecure, extremely interested in boys at a very early age, and very likely to become sexually active before age sixteen.

The Manipulator

RECIPE: Take one pushover father who doesn't follow through well on providing firm guidelines and limits for his daughter. He regards caving in to his daughter's demands as a sign of love or as the way females should be treated in general.
RESULT: A girl who has learned to use her femininity as a weapon to get her own way. Depending on the situation, she can flirt, pout, cry, tease, or flatter the males in her life to do as she pleases. This may be seen as cute at age six but not at sixteen or twenty-six.

The Turtle

RECIPE: Take one overprotective father who feels girls need shelter more than anything else. He is good at finishing the sentences she begins and pointing out her mistakes in early en-

deavors. Over time, he will be seen as limiting her possibilities because girls "can't do this" or "can't do that."
RESULT: A girl who is in her "shell" most of the time. She is afraid to try something new, feels insecure, and is reluctant to express her feelings.

The way we fathers normally treat our daughters is something we learned from how our fathers treated our mothers and sisters. That model may be positive or negative. If we realize we are in the process of reproducing a negative pattern, there are two practical steps we can take to learn a better approach: *Encouragement* and *Engagement*.

Encouragement

We should be our daughters' biggest and most enthusiastic fans.

One of the kids in the youth group is part of the "Red Flyers" cross-country running team. There is a girl on the team who comes in first in every run of every cross-country meet. Her father is a good example of a man who is interested in her activities. Unfortunately, he is an amazingly bad example of carrying something too far. When she wins, he wants to know why her time wasn't faster. When she runs along the road, he drives beside her and yells at her to push harder. He criticizes her constantly. He has Olympic hopes for this girl. Time will tell what will result from this high-demand and high-criticism approach.

Tom, on the other hand, made a decision when he held Jennifer as a baby: "I will compliment and affirm this girl every day of her life from today through high school graduation."

It wasn't easy. Jennifer turned out to be a very strong-willed child and teenager. She wanted the universe to be arranged to her precise requirements. If something didn't measure up, every-one knew.

"Hello, is this Mr. Tom Falkin? I'm sorry to inform you that your daughter Jennifer was discovered smoking marijuana awhile ago. We need you to come and get her." Tom, a church elder, wept as he drove the two hours to the church camp.

Through good times and bad, Tom kept his promise. Every day, even the darkest, even the day he had to pick her up from camp, he affirmed Jennifer for something. She, of course, figured out that this was his policy. She confided to him at age twenty-one, "Dad, even when I was being a brat, I still looked forward to what good you would say to me that day. You never failed. I knew you loved me and that God loved me too."

Tom's commitment to be an encourager saved their relation-ship.

While encouragement can't guarantee eighteen trouble-free years of growing up, it does build a daughter's self-esteem and confirms in her your love and the love of her Heavenly Father.

Engagement

I love electric trains. I love electric race-car sets too. When my oldest daughter, MaryAnn, turned two, to celebrate the big occasion I bought her . . . ah . . . make that, I bought *us* an electric train. When she turned seven, we got the race-car set. All of my daughters have enjoyed these "boy" toys with me.

In fathering, engagement means time together. Quality time and quality conversation are not easy to schedule. They happen serendipitously in the context of doing something together. In a father-daughter relationship, it is important to include your daughter in your interests—even if it is not a traditional "girl" interest. Fishing, computers, sports of all kinds, auto repair, real estate investment . . . if you are interested in these, you need to invite your daughter to become involved with you.

Social science research is publicizing that men are not very good when it comes to spending time with daughters. Most dads do extra things with sons but not with daughters. And while mothers tend to take both sons and daughters when they go somewhere, dads just take sons.[3]

One thing I am enjoying with my three girls (now ages fourteen, twelve, and eleven) this year is reading out loud together a book about mechanical things.[4] We have plumbed the depths of mysteries such as rack-and-pinion steering, transmissions, single lens reflex cameras, and photocopy machines—all as they relate to Woolly Mammoths. Sure, it sounds a little silly, but this weekly "How Things Work" session is a highlight for all of us.

As dads, we have the chance to be encouragers to our daughters as well as friends and mentors. Yes, we should be this with our sons too, but some men don't even consider being friends and mentors to their girls. It is something we can learn to do with a deep sense of fulfillment.

When it comes to daughters many fathers face a crisis when their daughters begin dating. You may feel a sense of loss, fear, even jealousy. You were once the "main man" in her life, but now it looks as if you've been knocked off this top spot. It is normal for a teenage girl not to want to talk with or share with her dad. She has her girlfriends to talk to. If she has a steady boyfriend, he gets to hear her hopes and fears before you do.

The commitment to encouragement and engagement should continue through the teenage years. There will be changes in the relationship, however. You'd better knock before opening her bedroom door. Wrestling and other full body contact father-daughter horseplay is out. Show your affection by a hand on the shoulder, a pat on the back, a kiss on the cheek, and eye contact.

It is important not to criticize your daughter's body. Some girls develop early, others late. Be assured your daughter is painfully aware of her body. Most teenage girls feel something is wrong with their bodies: too fat, too skinny, too something. Let your own not-so-little girl know that you think she looks fine.

Lyricist Oscar Hammerstein said, in effect, you can have fun with a son, but you have to father a daughter. You can have fun with a daughter too, but for most of us it takes awhile to learn the skills to father a daughter successfully. How about sons?

Fathers and Sons

Boys may spend more time with their moms, but they model more after their fathers. A boy looks to his dad to figure out how to get along, carry himself, and how to relate to the opposite sex. This modeling happens, for better or worse. Consider the following cases, all Christian fathers, active in their churches:

Most friends breathed a sigh of relief when the divorce was finalized. Floyd learned how to express anger from his dad, who yelled frequently and expressed his rage by being rough with his wife and five children. Floyd, the youngest of the five, had to endure this rage and abuse from his dad and his two older brothers. Floyd's wife, long-suffering for years, began plotting divorce the night he put his fist through the bedroom wall. She had begun going to a support group and learned that men who rage like this are sick and almost nothing cures this violence.

Martin is very quiet for a sixteen-year-old. He reacts to pressure by going inward. His feelings are not obvious to anyone. For sixteen years, his father has been silently teaching him that this is how to live: come home, eat supper, and go downstairs to watch TV. In conflict or pressure, silence and avoidance are the standard response. His life is a quiet combination of going to work, sitting in front of the TV, and twice a week driving to church.

There is something in Mike's smile that makes you like him. He is kind, interested, and confident without being cocky. Paul, his father, is an executive in the rarified air of upper management and is sometimes called "butter lips" by his associates. Paul always has the right thing to say, at the right time, with the right demeanor. He's no fake. He's not paying personal-favor dues by being nice. He likes people and sincerely cares. Paul has led two of his upper-management friends to Christ in the last twelve months. Mike, a university student, is patiently tearing down the misconceptions and barriers his roommate has about Christianity.

Three Christian men and three sons . . . for better or worse, the older is reproducing in the younger what he is like.

Wasn't it humbling the first time you saw something of you in your son?

"I nearly fainted when my three-year-old said, 'Oh, crap!' when he dropped a toy. My wife nailed me with the words, 'Any guess as to where he got that from, dear?' I've started to watch my language, that's for sure!"

Learning by Watching Others

We can learn how to be better fathers to our sons by watching the pros and cons of other father-son relationships. While no two fathers and no two sons are exactly alike, it's not hard to find similarities when we compare ourselves with others.

Famous child psychologist Dr. Lee Salk, brother of the developer of the polio vaccine, Jonas, set out across the country to interview men about their fathers. The result of his research is a book filled with real-life insight into what sons think about their dads. As you scan these names, occupations, and memory synopses, ask yourself this: What would my son say about me?

Hal, retailer: My dad was there . . . not warm, but at least available.

Richard, surveyor: I felt closest when we built something together.

David, publisher: I am absent much of the time as my dad was, but I still try to show that I love and care for my kids.

Weldon, forester: He always let me voice my opinion.

W.C., executive: I loved all the time we hunted and fished together.

Gerard, publisher: My father was a grim, burdened man.

Almet, engineer: He is my friend. He was a strict disciplinarian, but he was affectionate too.

George, bartender: My dad was always on my side, no matter what.

Fred, contractor: He was a workaholic. I wish we had spent more time together.

Patrick, construction supervisor: My father was not capable of expressing physical tenderness.

Mark, convicted murderer: He never told me he loved me, never apologized for anything.

Chris, gay, unemployed: There was no closeness between us. Even though he lived at home, a relationship didn't really exist.[5]

Sobering, isn't it? We remember our fathers and how they were toward us. Should we view the two-decade-long process of raising a son in only one way, or is it more realistic to look for stages?

Three Stages in Raising a Boy to Be a Man

A normal, healthy, and positive father-son relationship will proceed through three phases.

1. Close Emotional Relationship (Birth to 12)   A good father-son relationship will be the boy and dad really enjoying each other. The son will look up to his dad, and the dad will be proud of the development of the son. Yes, Dad may have to learn how to be devoted (chapter 2), but it can be done and will be thoroughly appreciated. Fatherhood, seen as a calling, becomes a priority as a man realizes he has only one shot at raising this son.

2. *Transition: The Struggle for Independence (Ages 13 to 19)* In chapter 9 we will discuss how parents can actually be friends with kids in the teenage years. It is absolutely normal, even in the best father-son relationship, for there to be some stress.

Face it: the purpose of adolescence is for the son (or daughter) to move from total dependence to total independence. To do this, you must gradually let go, sector by sector, of direct control of your son's life.

My father, in one wise pronouncement, eliminated 99 percent of the problems many fathers and sons have. When I was sixteen, he handed me the keys to the car he had bought me and said, "Leonard, if I ever hear that you are showing off or driving fast or getting in trouble with this car, we'll park it till you're eighteen . . . no excuses, no nothing. I trust you, though, and from here on you have no curfew, you don't have to check in; we know you want to please the Lord, and that makes us feel comfortable giving you your freedom."

My dad gave me complete freedom, at age sixteen, conditional on my continued responsible behavior. I was so grateful, I wanted more than ever to please him, as well as my Heavenly Father. I had an added incentive: lots of my friends were in constant conflict with their parents over driving, being out late, and irresponsibility. I could see that approach was a total dead end.

3. *Man-to-Man Friends (Age 20 +)*[6]   Many sons come to appreciate their dads at a deeper level when they move away from home. They realize how much real work and real money it takes to pay for shelter, food, insurance, and all the rest. They may or may not come back for our advice and input. If you have

had a good relationship through the teen years, the friendship can be deep and profound as your son gets into his twenties. One father, reflecting on a recent visit from his son, told me, "I never thought it could be this good."

Talking to Boys About Sex

I'll be the first to admit it: having three daughters means this is an issue I know almost nothing about. I say "almost" because I do recall how I got a sex education: from school, from my junior high friends, and from my mother. About age twelve, I began asking her some embarrassing questions. She came home with a book and left it on my bed.

Therefore, I'd like to lean on a father who is teaching his boys about sex. Author Steve Farrar recommends the following principles:

1. Small questions deserve small answers.
2. Big questions deserve big answers.
3. Frank questions deserve frank answers.
4. Be casual and natural.
5. Look for teachable moments.
6. Use the right terms without embarrassment.
7. Consider the age of the child.
8. Let him know he can ask you anything and get a straight answer. [7]

For a book-length treatment of parents teaching kids about sex, I highly recommend *Decent Exposure: How to Teach Your Kids About Sex* by Connie Marshner (Wolgemuth & Hyatt, 1988).

Raising daughters, raising sons . . . we can learn to tailor our fathering to each of these very special relationships. What about trying to father when our work schedule means we travel?

Fathers On the Move

Executives travel. Even though these are the days of teleconferencing, satellite video conferences, info over fiber optics and fast fax, every day hundreds of thousands of American men and women get on planes (or climb into cars) and travel to get things done. It is reported that upscale executives commuting between Los Angeles and New York/Washington, D.C., have a term for the rest of us. We are *fly-over people*. These hotshots, while busy running the country, just fly over the rest of us while we go about our daily grind.[8] While they commute between the coasts, we stay glued to boring jobs in boring places.

Well, even fly-over people travel in the course of our jobs. Many business travelers face another reality. The week before we travel has extra pressure as we get ready. The week after we get back is crazy as we face a desk that begs us to rent a front-end loader or bulldozer to clean it off. As fathers, the question becomes this: How do we communicate care when we can't be there? Additionally, how do we appear "normal" with out kids in the rush before we leave and the crunch that comes after?

I have had to give this one some major-league attention. While I'm not a CEO or other high executive in the business world, my travel schedule as a youth pastor is as filled as many of theirs. As I ponder this schedule, I thank the Lord for the joy of ministry and the creative fun it is to communicate care to my family even when I'm not around physically. Yet I face this schedule with a mix of joy and sadness. Here is the year: four weekend retreats with the youth groups plus four additional one-night retreats or conferences; two pastors' meetings at four overnights each; and an additional twenty-one nights away at speaking or teaching engagements in Regina, Calgary, New York, and San Diego. This is tame compared with some men I know, but suffice it to say, I've had to work at being a good dad though I am absent some of the time.

Communicating Care When We're Not There

Here are ten ideas. I've used them all. They are not the last word . . . think of others that fit your style.

Bringing Something Back   My dad used this one; I do too. A little souvenir or something from the hotel room (not towels!) will delight a child. I don't bring my girls souvenirs anymore. If I receive an honorarium for speaking or teaching, after tithe and taxes, a good portion of the money goes for something special for the kids: horse camp, a concert, or something else our normal family budget doesn't fund . . . my girls really appreciate these.

Cards and Letters   If I'm going to be gone more than four nights, I start writing cards or letters on my first night. It's fun to forage for funny cards in trendy places.

Delivery Surprises   It is really fun to blow your family away with a singing flower telegram. I've asked friends to make a special dinner for the family and bring it over on a certain night. I tell my wife in advance not to prepare anything because I'm in charge of the meal that night. When people do this for us, they tend to go all out . . . my kids love it.

Joint Projects   For this one, agree with a son or daughter to read the same chapter of Scripture or same chapter of book on the same day. This can then be discussed via letter, phone, or when you get back.

Kindness and Gifts   If I'm gone longer than a weekend, I try to leave a bag of surprises for each girl (including my wife). Here's a typical five-day surprise bag:

Day 1: Candy.

Day 2: A funny card.

Day 3: A drawing of some recent family memory. (My drawing

is so bad, these pictures become the source of much hilarity in our home.

Day 4: Animal-shaped bath soap or a novelty toy.

Day 5: A mushy card. (Girls, remember?)

Notes   Similar to the last suggestion. Just leave notes of kindness and affirmation around where they will be discovered.

Phone   Be sure not to call when your wife is making supper or at a bad time for your kids!

Take Them With You   This can be a father-son or a father-daughter highlight. If you travel enough to join an airline mileage club, do it. Use the free ticket you earn to take a kid. Among my best memories ever are taking each of my kids, in turn, with me to New York.

Video or Audiocassette Recording   When my kids were little, this was a favorite. Before my trip, I would prerecord two audio segments for each day.

Typical morning segment:

1. Wake-up song (I'm a terrible singer!).
2. Guess-the-weather game.
3. What I'm doing that day.
4. The Scripture verse of the day.

Typical evening segment:

1. Speculation about their day.
2. Bedtime story reading.
3. Evening prayer.

Treasure Hunt   It's fun to lead the family from clue to clue, room to room, with a prize of candy, money, or flowers. The clues can be done on audio or videotape or with notes in envelopes. The mantel, the ceiling, and under a bed all make great clue-stashing places.

Avoiding the Rush and Crunch

Rush and crunch are almost impossible to avoid. I have accepted this as a given. My decision as a dad, however, is to be both disciplined and smart about it. By God's grace I try to minimize the impact my travel has on the family.

In the pressured week prior to and the week after travel, I am extra careful to "leave my work at the line" as I drive home. This imaginary boundary line my tires cross on the commute home signals my mental transfer from office (with its problems) to home and my family.

If my desk work is piled high and needs to be cleared out, I try to work the extra time when my family doesn't normally see me anyway. On Wednesday nights, for example, my meetings are over about 9:30 P.M. Sometimes I've stayed until midnight clearing out the backlog of desk work. If morning seems a better time, the alarm will go off at the normal time for running. Instead, though, I'm off to the office. It's amazing how much can be accomplished before 8:30 in the morning or after 9:30 at night.

My goal in all of this is to have a normal family schedule and not make my wife and kids suffer because of a work-caused crunch.

When we really think about it, there are many different special considerations we fathers face. Father-son, father-daughter, and hectic travel can all be triggers for creativity and growth in our learning to be better dads.

What about being a dad to a teenager? "Can anything good come out of Nazareth?" we may rhetorically ask. And also, how can one better handle a remarried family situation?

Questions for Discussion

1. Do you know any girls who seemed to be completely transformed for the worse in adolescence?

2. Are you in the process of making your daughter "young and sexy," a "manipulator," or a "turtle"?

3. Think of some father-son relationships you know about. In what ways are the boys turning out like or unlike their fathers?

4. Twenty years from now, how do you think your son might describe his relationship with you as it stands now?

5. If you travel for business, what impact is this having on your family?

6. What additional ideas can you suggest to communicate care when you are away on business, or which of the author's ideas seems most workable to you?

7. Open your Bible and read Psalm 116:1-7. With which of these seven verses do you most identify in your role as a dad right now?

Idea Corner 8

Ten ideas for caring when you can't be there are given on pages 147–149.

Special Considerations 2

Father-Teenager
Single Fathering
The Remarried Family

I have already told you my wife, Janet, and I hiked, back-packed, and camped our way through our first two months of married life. You'd think after being engaged for 509 days, there wouldn't be too many surprises after the big day arrived. Wrong.

I was shocked to discover, and nearly two decades of subsequent married life have amply confirmed, that mosquitoes are attracted to my wife. No kidding. We step out of the car onto the trail and she's counting the bites within minutes. I—and this is no kidding too—don't get bitten. If Ms. Mosquito lands on me at all, she does two things: (1) pauses briefly in hesitant uncertainty and (2) buzzes off for better prey (usually Janet, if she's within fifty yards).

The mystery was solved this morning. My eyes widened and I

called to my wife as I read, "Mosquitoes *are* partial to certain people. Their preferences appear to be dictated by biochemical factors. Mosquitoes are drawn to carbon dioxide and amino acids . . . respiratory and metabolic by-products that are given off in different amounts by different people. . . ."[1]

Now I can affirm her, during our next outdoor adventure, on just how special and unique she is. It's a specialness she'd rather not be blessed with, but apparently she has no choice.

In fathering, we may find ourselves in special situations that might not be ideal, but we are there nonetheless. Let's look at three of these special situations: being a dad to teens, fathering in a remarried family, and being a single dad.

Being a Dad to Teenagers

Twice in the last seven days, I have had the fun of making a statement that made people gawk at me in disbelief.

"It's just so great to have a teenager in the home. My wife and I have been looking forward to this for a long time, and it's everything we hoped it would be. We've got two more on the verge, and we're excited about their becoming teenagers too."

My bank teller put our transaction on hold, rested her hands on the counter, and slowly raised her eyes to meet mine. We had been making small talk and I don't remember what triggered my teenager statement. This woman had seen me dozens of times, but her now wide eyes were studying me.

"You never hear *anyone* say that about teenagers."

I replied, "Another thing I'm excited about is that our oldest will be driving soon."

Her mouth dropped open, and she resumed our transaction without saying another word.

Next week, I'll try to get her window again and mention something about the difference God makes in our family life. Chances are she won't pass me off as a Bible-thumping zealot.

Being a dad to teenagers doesn't have to be all stress and struggle. Let's face squarely, as fathers, three crucial issues: discipline, communication, and friendship.

Disciplining Teenagers: What Works, What Doesn't

Tom walks through the kitchen in a rush. Only fifteen minutes before it's time to leave for an elders special meeting at church. He got up that Saturday morning promising his wife, "Dear, I'll fix the shelf in the den today, you can count on it."

The day went so quickly, and now it's almost time to leave. Mary, his wife, is studying for a night class and he assures her, "Don't worry, dear, it will take only ten minutes. I'll have it done before I leave for church."

Tom walks into the garage, flips the light on, and faces the workbench. Metal brace? In hand. Box of wood screws? In hand. Cordless screwdriver? There's an empty place where it normally hangs. Calmly at first, then with more urgency, Tom hunts for the tool, first in the garage, then elsewhere in the house. Ten minutes pass and still no success in the search.

On his way back to the garage, Tom hears a car pull up and opens the garage door.

"Hi Dad," son Pete exclaims. "How's your day going?"

"Pete, do you have the power screwdriver?"

"Sure thing, it's right here in the backseat. I needed it this morning when I took out those old speakers. Sorry I forgot to put it back."

"You bet you're sorry!" Tom yells. "If I've told you once I've told you a million times to put the tools away. You're so irresponsible I just don't know what to do. I don't know what you had planned for the rest of the weekend, but you're grounded, boy, you're stationary, on restriction in your room, understand? I just can't tolerate this any longer!"

How will Tom's son respond, do you think? Will he cheerfully

obey, abandoning his weekend plans, and go to his room thinking of ways he can show his sincere repentance to his dad? As he
gently shuts his door will he say to himself, *Gee, I'm so lucky to
have a dad who helps me see my failings?*

Maybe one sixteen-year-old son in ten thousand will respond
this way, but the vast majority won't.

High-volume anger, a minilecture, labeling, and restriction
are not exactly productive responses when a teenage son or
daughter errs.

In late 1989 and early 1990, I asked nearly four hundred
college-age Christian students all over North America to reflect
on the discipline they had received at home in early, middle, and
late adolescence. The results of that research formed the basis of
my book *Teen Shaping: Solving the Discipline Dilemma* (Fleming
H. Revell Company, 1990).

Take a moment and fill out the following questionnaire, which
originally appeared in *Teen Shaping:*

Style of Parenting Questionnaire

*Part I When a situation arises that requires me to discipline my son
or daughter, I . . .*

	never	occasionally	usually
1. raise my voice.	_____	_____	_____
2. announce the punishment and do not allow discussion.	_____	_____	_____

	never	occasionally	usually
3. expect 100 percent compliance with my wishes in the matter.	_____	_____	_____
4. basically ignore the explanation or excuses my kid offers.	_____	_____	_____
5. believe my opinion is right most of the time.	_____	_____	_____
6. explain fully the reason discipline is appropriate.	_____	_____	_____
7. ask questions to help clarify the situation.	_____	_____	_____
8. let my kid have a say in the discipline.	_____	_____	_____

	never	ocassionally	usually
9. seriously consider his or her input and opinion on the matter.	_____	_____	_____
10. change my mind or reduce the discipline I had decided upon based on input from my son or daughter.	_____	_____	_____
11. would not normally say anything about it.	_____	_____	_____
12. have no opinion on the given behavior of my kid.	_____	_____	_____
13. ignore the situation.	_____	_____	_____
14. feel it is not my place to give out discipline at this age.	_____	_____	_____

	never	occasionally	usually
15. have very few expectations about the behavior of my kids.	_____	_____	_____

Part II I try to . . .

1. hug or touch my kids.

2. make myself available to listen to my kids' problems.	_____	_____	_____
3. express appreciation to him or her.	_____	_____	_____
4. affirm my kids when they do something well.	_____	_____	_____
5. spend quality time with my kids every week, where we really interact.	_____	_____	_____

Scoring, Part I

Draw a line between questions 5 and 6 as well as between questions 10 and 11.

Questions 1–5: Number of "usually" responses: _____

Questions 6–10: Number of "usually" responses: _____

Questions 11–15: Number of "usually" responses: _____

In any section (1–5, 6–10, 11–15), indicating "usually" three or more times would suggest this is your normal parenting style. The authoritarian or autocratic style is indicated by a high "usually" score on questions 1–5. Equalitarian or democratic style is the preference shown by a high "usually" in questions 6–10. Permissive or ignoring is indicated by the same in 11–15.

Scoring, Part II

This brief section has to do with the level of "nurturance" you, as a father, provide your young person.

Score 3 for every "usually" marked _____

Score 1 for every "occasionally" marked _____

Obviously, the higher your score, the more nurturing you are.

0–5: Urgent need for improvement

6–10: Okay, but lots of room for improvement

11–15: Excellent

Now that we have identified our general parenting style, what does it really mean, and what effect does this have when it comes to discipline?

The *autocratic or authoritarian* are "high control" approaches to fathering. They are styles in which adolescents are not allowed to express opinions or make decisions about any aspect of their own lives. Less severe but still high control is when young people can contribute opinions but we as fathers always make the final decision according to our own judgment.[2]

My research for *Teen Shaping* showed that this high-control style was 87 percent effective with eleven- to thirteen-year-olds, 58 percent effective with fourteen- to sixteen-year-olds, and 37 percent effective with seventeen- to nineteen-year-olds. Clearly, it works pretty well when the kids are younger, especially if combined with high nurture.

Hang on to high-control fathering too long, however, and you are likely to produce (1) a tension-filled home, (2) rebellious and aloof teenagers who have little regard for your values and beliefs, (3) teens who learn to become masters at lying and covert behavior, and finally, (4) sons and daughters who are ripe for a peer-pressure-induced fall, since they feel so little support at home.

I could fill a chapter, if not a whole book, with sad-but-true cases of fathers who clung to a high-control approach and lost their kids in the process.

The *permissive or ignoring* approaches are "low control." This style of fathering means the adolescent assumes a more active and influential position in formulating decisions, considering but not always abiding by parental opinions. Low control carried to the extreme is one in which the father takes no role and evidences no interest in directing the adolescent's behavior.

Research shows that the permissive/ignoring style tends to produce young people who have low self-esteem, feel alienated, and are highly likely to have trouble with alcohol or drugs. They are also prone to "standard-breaking behavior."[3] That is, they are crying out for attention and go to extremes to get it. The problem with the overpermissive or ignoring father is not that of too much discipline but not enough. Young people want to feel loved and cared for. Especially in early adolescence, they are searching for behavioral boundary lines. Don't believe it? Ask a kid what he or she thinks about a teacher at school who doesn't have control of the class. Sure, it's fun the first few days, but then many will feel frustrated that their time is being wasted.

The *democratic or equalitarian* approaches are midpoint between the above two extremes. In the democratic style, adolescents contribute freely to the discussion of issues relevant to their behavior and make some of their own decisions, but final decisions are often formulated by the father (or mother) and are always subject to his approval. The equalitarian style is one in which parents and teens play essentially similar roles and participate equally in making decisions.

My research for *Teen Shaping* showed the success of this approach is dramatically different from the high-control style of fathering once past age thirteen.

With eleven- to thirteen-year-olds: 80 percent

With fourteen- to sixteen-year-olds: 80 percent

With seventeen- to nineteen-year-olds: 90 percent

In this style of fathering, the young person feels the respect and value of his or her dad. When we, as men, feel respected, we are motivated in a positive way. It's no different for kids.[4] Another reason this style fosters maturity is that rules and discipline are explained calmly instead of commanded. The democratic approach takes the time to help the young person see why misbehavior hurts the son or daughter.[5]

This ought to really make us think: national studies have shown that the democratic or equalitarian style of parenting also produces self-esteem, ability to get along with others, a desire to succeed, ownership of positive moral values, and concern for others. It produces kids who are far less likely to feel alienated, hostile, or have the need to become involved in substance abuse.[6]

If we are using a high-control approach to fathering with our early adolescents, when should we begin to loosen up?

Steve Miller sits in his favorite chair in the family room. Over the top of his paper he can see his twelve-year-old daughter and fourteen-year-old son doing their homework at the kitchen table. Somewhere around page two of the sports section, his attention is diverted.

William: I think it's wrong that we let Japan sell its products so freely here, and they don't let us do the same over there.

Jill: But put yourself in their shoes. I read an article that said they really believe they want to protect their way of life. Cheap American rice will put their farmers out of business.

William: But what about. . . .

Steve chuckles to himself. Only in the last six months or so have his kids occasionally had this kind of sophisticated discussion. "I feel as if I'm listening to a debate on National Public Radio or something."

What Steve is enjoying is that both his kids can think about a thought. That is, they can take an idea, even a complex, many-faceted one, and wander around it in their heads. This ability engages in the female brain at about ages eleven to thirteen. Boys are a little slower. William, at age fourteen, is ahead of his peers, as most boys come on-line mentally at around age sixteen.

If we're smart, we'll "go democratic" if we're not already when our kids start to gain this ability to think abstractly. There is an immense amount of brainpower coming on-line and it wants to be respected, trusted, and utilized.

I love teaching junior high school kids. It's so much fun to see the vast difference between boys and girls when it comes to brainpower. Most girls can talk about spiritual things and show real insight. Most boys . . . well, the lights are on but no one is home.

A democratic style of fathering is made a lot easier if we improve at communication.

Getting Better at Making Connection

Yesterday, I really messed up. I'm ashamed to admit it, since I teach and write about this so much, but my slip illustrates how hard it is to change a cemented habit. What happened?

We were having family devotions. It was prayer-request time. My daughter sat bolt upright on the sofa, put her knuckles to her hips, and exclaimed, "I'm so mad that at camp next week we have to have play practice for ninety minutes each morning."

Being the all-wise, expert, and insightful father I am, I calmly replied, "But think of all the fun you'll have doing that. I know you like working on the play."

My wife, ever vigilant, coughed and laughed out loud as my daughter said, "But Dad! I'd rather be running in the woods, or looking for crabs at the beach, or searching for snakes in the grass."

I knew as soon as the words were out of my mouth that I had done it *again!* What had I done? I had violated the number-one rule, the primary principle, the cornerstone concept of parent-kid communication. Here's the rule I so blatantly broke:

> *When your kid shares a hurt/need/frustration . . .*
> *don't give advice first!*

Did my nickel's worth of advice make my daughter feel comforted, heard, or helped? No. It increased her frustration. She didn't need my advice. She needed to know that she was heard and understood.

With a smile at my wife, I turned to my daughter and said, "Hilary, I'm really sorry for not listening to you first. I made a mistake. So, it sounds like the play practice at camp is a real disappointment, right?

"Yeah, and. . . ." Our conversation was off and running.

As adults, as men, we have this inner compulsion to instantly answer the issues/needs presented us by our young people. Children and teenagers (and wives too!) don't want or need our advice first. They need our understanding. They need to know their feelings have been acknowledged. Our instant advice is often received as a put-down, and it slams the door to communication.

After we have listened and drawn out the feelings and thoughts, then it may be appropriate to give advice and to offer counsel.

It's tough to wiggle out of advice-giving cement shoes. If we don't, however, our relationship with a teenage son or daughter is likely to sink to the river bottom. How I've tried to wiggle out is by (1) being aware and (2) encouraging Janet to let me know when she hears me blow it.

If we master this, we're well on our way to what proves to be the impossible dream for too many fathers.

Being a Friend to Your Teenagers and Their Friends

If we find it difficult to appreciate the importance of our teenagers' friends, we will do well to make the effort to recall our own feelings about friends in junior and senior high school. Take a moment now to reflect on the friends you had as a teenager.

1. How important were these friends to you?
2. How much time did you spend with them or want to spend with them?
3. If your father tried to restrict access to your friends, what was your reaction, and what did the efforts of your father accomplish?

Here is another question to ponder: When you were a teen-ager, did you have any adults you considered your friend? If so, what are three good characteristics you recall about them? List your recollections here:

1.
2.
3.

Chances are good that you listed things such as, "Interested in me," "Fun to be around," "Enthusiastic about life."

These are very important to young people.

It's not easy, is it? We come home from a high-pressure, high-stress day jammed with demands and expectations. We come home tired, replaying the day. Being fun to be around and showing enthusiasm for life is not high on our agenda. We're in a recovery mode.

We may not be able to pull it off in the first hour home, but at least occasionally our kids should see us having fun, being fun, and sincerely enjoying them.

If we learn to do this and couple it with good communication, we will make progress in befriending our kids and their friends.

Three additional ideas will help us build bridges to our teen-agers' friends. First, remember when you meet a friend of your son or daughter for the very first time, you have only seven seconds to make your first impression. That's how long it takes before most of us "decide" on a person and, once we "decide," it takes a long time to change our minds.[7] Even if we're tired, even if we are mentally trying to backfill a day that's been dug full of holes, we need to smile sincerely, give good eye contact, and say a welcome in our own way.

Second, our home should be adolescent-friendly. If we want our kids to be home sometimes, and to bring their friends, then it must be equipped with things to do that kids like. As a youth pastor, I've seen hundreds of parents handle this in many ways: Ping-Pong or pool tables, sport courts, guaranteed full cookie jars, hot tubs, foosball tables, swimming pools, and state-of-the-art video games.

Third, show teenagers respect, not condescension. When daughter Julie brings home a friend, ask Julie's friend for her opinion on something. Would she recommend a Ford or a Chevy? Does she think it's easier to brush, roll, or spray cedar siding? How would she solve the mess down at city hall? Don't jump all over friends with these questions, but offer questions casually, with a sincere attitude. Listen well. If possible, follow the advice given. If we practice these three ideas, we will find ourselves learning to be better dads to teenagers.

Being a dad to teenagers is a special challenge and opportunity.

The Single Father

Nationally, 5 percent of single-parent families are headed by men.[8] That may not seem like many compared with families headed by women, but it still represents tens of thousands of households across the country where a man is trying to be both father and mother. Single parenting is not easy.

Fitzhugh Dodson, nationally recognized expert on families and on raising kids, recommends several steps crucial to survival if a man (or woman) is going to raise kids alone.

Make Sure You're in Charge

Kids realize that you, as a single father, have much on your mind. You work hard all day and then come home to do a second shift. It is easy for a son or daughter, especially a strong-willed one, to pressure and hound you about food, bedtime, curfew, money, and the like. A strong-willed kid can almost smell weakness and vulnerability.

You must learn to assert that you are in charge, and let there be consequences if you don't get cooperation. A weekly family meeting is important to go over chores, iron out problems, and affirm good behavior. It is always nice if the family meeting can be ended with ice cream or something seen as good and fun by all.

Develop a Positive Reward System

It is so much better (and less time-consuming!) to reward the good than to fix the bad. Affirming words, notes, hugs, a special night out, extra privileges are all signs that you notice the good you see in your kids. Each time you affirm the good, you make its recurrence more likely.

Find a Surrogate Mother

This will help immensely, especially with daughters. Here the church can be of invaluable help, as a kind woman who loves kids can see your daughter as a way to serve God.[9] Girls need female role models.

Be Organized

A single father must manage his time with the expertness of a master conductor. With three active kids in the Kageler house, I am amazed at how complicated our schedule normally is. Fortunately for me, my wife manages the calendar and keeps us from going crazy. If I were a single father, I'd buy a big schedule board and a planner/organizer. Each day, some time would need to be given just to calendar planning and updating.

Deal With Guilt

Fathers who have become single via divorce will probably deal with the undertow of guilt. My friend Jack did everything humanly possible to save his troubled marriage. He prayed, sought counseling, and went numerous "extra miles" to reconcile with his wife. She, however, had decided she no longer wanted him, and there was nothing that would change her mind. Jack is by all accounts the "innocent party" in this tragedy, yet he still feels guilty. He wonders, *Is there something more I could have done? Something more I should have said?*

Again and again, Jack throws his heart and soul at the feet of the Lord, asking for strength. His head knows he's been forgiven for his mistakes, but his heart has not caught up with his head.

I have known several Jacks in my years as a pastor. It takes a very long time for the feelings of guilt to go away. False guilt is a tool of the Enemy to neutralize our ministries as men.

Make Time for Dad

One pothole that makes the ride bumpy for some single fathers is that they forget to take care of themselves. They serve others at work. Then they come home and all their energy goes into providing a good life for their kids. They give 100 percent at their jobs, 100 percent to their kids, and there is 0 percent left for themselves. It's a fast track to burnout and failure.

Single fathers need to *schedule* time for refreshment. Without this infusion of restoring time, the life gets sucked out of them until they have nothing left to give.

While single fathers may be comparatively few, many more live in remarried family situations.

The Remarried Family

We all know a remarried family, right? There are more than 13 million family units in the U.S. where at least one partner had been previously married and brought children to the marriage. That means 13 million stepfathers, trying for better or worse to make family life work for them.[10] Stepfathering or

"Brady Bunch" blended-family fathering is a major challenge.

What are some of the time bombs that begin ticking when a remarried family is created?

The Ideal of the "Normal Family"

One myth is that a remarried family can and should feel like an ideal normal family not long after the wedding. You may feel, as the father, that now everything should be just fine in the eyes of every family member. Not so.

Research is showing that it takes children two years to feel bonded in a remarried family. Some children, while finally feeling a sense of stability after two years, never achieve meaningful bonding with the stepparent. Girls especially have a difficult time giving loyalty to a stepfather. In many cases, they feel a continuing loyalty to the biological father and conclude that giving loyalty to a second father is a betrayal of the first.[11]

This pressure to make the family "feel close" can put a major strain on the new marriage.

Family Executives

The power structure in a normal family is (1) parents (who are the executives), (2) children, and (3) pets. When a remarried family is made, there are initial questions as to who the executives are. "I don't have to mind you 'cause you're not my real dad!" is a statement many stepfathers have heard. Another common scenario is that a stepson or stepdaughter receives a directive from the stepfather and then checks its validity with the mother.

Both husband and wife have to have good bonding and good agreement on family rules for there to be harmony in the home. As the kids see this stability and mutual trust, it will help them feel secure.

One of the best ways to succeed at stepfathering is to not force yourself on your stepchildren. Be kind, supportive, and affirming. Watch for clues as to what these new kids enjoy and what they are interested in. As they become more comfortable with you, you can begin to participate with them in areas of their interest. Especially with teenagers, you have no authority until you have a relationship, and the best doorway to a relationship is common interest.

I have said almost nothing in these chapters of the pain that comes with being a dad. Whether blending families, single fathering, or partnering with a wonderful wife, being a father is a bumpy road to travel at its very best. Let's look now at how we cope with the pain and disappointment that so easily comes to us as dads.

Questions for Discussion

1. What kind of parenting style did your father use when you were eleven to thirteen? Did it change as you grew older? How?

2. According to the parenting style questionnaire, which is your style of usual choice? How did you score on nurturing? Are any changes appropriate in your style or nurture level?

3. How prone are you to giving quick advice when your son or daughter shares a need or frustration?

4. How is your relationship with your kids' friends?

5. If there are any single dads or stepdads in your group, have them share one or two of the greatest struggles they face as fathers.

6. Open your Bibles and read James 3:13–18. In verse 17, which of the characteristics of wisdom do you feel most in need of today?

Idea Corner 9

With Preschoolers

Have you been to the library with your preschooler yet? Some libraries have toys and play areas for children to enjoy while the parents search for fun books to bring home. Many libraries include a film or video section. Check out a movie projector and screen, select some cartoons or animal programs, and you're set for an evening of entertainment.

With Elementary Age

You've got some interests or hobbies, right? Let your children help you. Are you into working on your house or yard? Have them help paint a fence. Do you like to bike? So do kids! Are you a model boat builder or judo expert? Your kids will enjoy doing this with you.

With Teenagers

Remember pen pals? Find an area of the world you and your teenager are interested in—perhaps even interested enough to try to visit someday. Ask around among the social studies teachers or at the public library for how you can get a pen pal in that country. Sit down together and write your first letter. You'll enjoy getting the reply and building a long-distance relationship.

The Wounded Father

At an early age, we learn things don't always turn out the way we expect.

I was at a track meet just the other day to watch my girls in their spring sport. Usually I bring along *The Atlantic* or a book to pass the time between events. It was a mild afternoon, and I was fully submerged in an article about the Soviet economy (or lack thereof). My attention was distracted by the gun sounding for the fifty-yard dash, and I looked up to see eight boys, ages seven and eight, bursting from the starting line.

With arms flailing and legs churning, they sped for the finish line. The boy in seventh place was several inches smaller than his peers. He looked like a five-year-old, yet there he was, with stress-contoured face, just a foot behind the sixth-place runner. In the last fifteen yards, though, things changed dramatically. Sixth place opened his lead to three yards, and in the final distance, the last-place boy passed the little boy I had been watching so intently.

Realizing he had just finished in eighth place out of eight, he stopped just a yard after the finish line and, oblivious to the crowd, he turned toward us, put his fists to his eyes, and started to cry. His chest heaved as he sobbed and sobbed. It got very quiet in the bleachers. Everyone froze as this boy's big tears streamed down his face, and we heard the sound of a heart that was breaking. It seemed like five minutes, but it was only about twenty seconds before his coach came over with a comforting arm.

That pitiful instant brought tears to my eyes too. *Well, little guy*, I thought, *welcome to the cold, cruel world. You ain't seen nothin' yet.*

The experience of this little boy is, for so many, a picture of fatherhood. You think you're doing okay . . . sure, you're not the best father on the planet, but you are trying hard. You think your kids are going to get through childhood and the teenage years without becoming alcoholic, being addicted to drugs, or getting pregnant. You can see the finish, it's almost there, and then, *wham.* All of a sudden, you realize your kid is out of control. Like getting too close to a blast furnace, your heart gets singed as you realize the unhappy truth.

Fathers get burned. Fathers get wounded. We find our hopes and dreams for our kids dashed to smithereens on the rocks of reality. So much of us, all the years of parenting, our reputation and self-respect so easily get shot out of the sky and crash on the tarmac of willful misbehavior.

Feeling Wounded? You're Not Alone

Let's listen in on some fathers comparing their fatherhood crises.

Jim: It was after supper. I was reading the paper and watching the news. My daughter, Karen, had been quiet all during supper, and my son, Mike, looked as if he'd been hit by a train. I found out Karen had told him the night before. After the dishwasher was loaded, Mike left the room and Karen told Sue and me she needed to talk.

Finally she blurted out, "I'm pregnant and I'm so scared" and burst into tears. I blew up. I hated her boyfriend. I had lectured and warned her. I yelled, "After all we've given you, this is what you do. Thanks a lot." I went downstairs to my office. I was so angry I honestly felt I could kill.

Sam: I felt angry too. My shock came when the police called and said they had my son, Jenkins, and his friend at the police station. They had been caught shoplifting at the mall.

Kevin: I thought everything was great with my boy until someone from the youth group called Mary to say they were concerned for him. We were told he was hanging with the wrong crowd and was sometimes drunk at school. I couldn't believe it. In fact, I didn't believe it. Not my boy. No, God wouldn't let that happen.

Sam: What happened then?

Kevin: I pushed it out of my mind for a couple of days. Then the vice-principal called me at work to say Tom was being suspended for three days for being drunk during class.

Larry: My situation seems tame compared with all of yours. But it hurts me so much, and that's why I'm here.

Jim: No pregnancy with your daughter, no jail for your son?

Larry: No, nothing like that. I guess what's tearing me up is that I thought the kids and I would be friends. I really thought it would work. I tried hard to keep in touch with them. Things were fine when they were kids, but after age fourteen it seemed as if both Lisa and Ben left, and two other kids I hardly even knew took their places. All of a sudden I wasn't on their list of priorities. They had no interest in spending time with me. They dutifully did their chores. They went to grandma's on Mother's Day. They weren't in open rebellion, but I could tell they were far, far away. I was an outsider, a stranger to them. This has been one of the biggest disappointments in my life.

These are hurting fathers. And they're not alone.

James Dobson surveyed thirty-five thousand families and came home with some sobering statistics. He found that, during the teenage years, 28 percent of young people rebelled severely.[1] Severe here means out of control and one or more of the following: alcohol abuse, drug abuse, crime, skipping school, running away, and other forms of out-of-control behavior. Of young people who were strong-willed (33 percent of the total surveyed), about 70 percent of them rebelled at least moderately in the teenage years.[2] Maybe there were no jail-term or drunk-at-school problems here, but they were problems big enough to present a major challenge to the parents.

Certainly strong-willed kids can break a parent's heart long before teendom arrives, but we can read into Dobson's statistics an immense amount of grief.

What are some normal reactions we fathers have when our kids take our carefully and neatly constructed world and blast it to bits?

Bad News Aftermath and Putting Life Back Together

If you have had, or are having, a kid-induced, broken-world experience, answer the following survey honestly.

In the aftermath of the crises with my son or daughter, I have felt or experienced the following (circle 1–5):

	No Feelings Like This				Very Intense Feelings
1. Anger	1	2	3	4	5
2. Doubting God or His goodness	1	2	3	4	5
3. Guilt	1	2	3	4	5
4. Self-doubt	1	2	3	4	5
5. Concern for my own reputation	1	2	3	4	5
6. Blaming	1	2	3	4	5
7. Stress in my marriage	1	2	3	4	5

If you score a 4 or 5 in more than a couple of these areas, you can call yourself a wounded father. Let's look at each one and consider some ways we can learn to heal.

Anger

Jim's daughter got pregnant. Jim got something too: angry. Anger, like overdone toast from an old toaster, pops up when we feel we've been burned. We, being human, like to have smooth sailing. Unfortunately, often our kids give no thought to our desire to cruise along without major storms. The serious misbehavior of our kids causes us to lose sleep. It may cost us great amounts of money as well: collision repairs, in-patient drug treatment, court-imposed restitution. The possibilities are nearly endless.

Behind much anger, I strongly believe, is fear.

Have you ever run over a dog? My semicomatose commute home from the office one day was rudely interrupted as I hit a dog. First there was a thud, then the car bounced up, and then I heard earsplitting yelping. That poor animal was very much alive but pinned underneath my transmission. I tried to get under the car to help, but the dog nearly bit off my arm. It was afraid, confused, and ready to attack all comers with its remaining strength.

Our kids have the power to nearly destroy our lives. When we are hit with a crisis and are pinned down by seemingly impossible circumstances, we can be afraid. We're afraid we are losing control. We're afraid of the future. We are fearful that this pain will never, ever, subside.

The first step toward healing is to express our anger to God. The Jews held captive in Babylon in the fifth century B.C. didn't hesitate to tell God the anger in their souls. Thinking about their captivity, they scream, "Blessed is he who takes your babies and dashes them against the rocks" (Psalm 137:9 my translation).

These people were wounded, and they vented their frustration on God. You know, God somehow manages to absorb our anger. I doubt if He has ever had a "bad day" because of any anger we have aimed in His holy direction.

A good second step is to read the Book of Job. Here is a dad who was wounded! No, his kids did not go bad; they were dead. All that remained of his family was his wife, who offered him little solace with the words, "Curse God and die!" (Job 2:9). In Job, Habakkuk, and other Scriptures, we are reminded that God is not obligated to answer our questions. Crisis kicks out all the props from under us. We are knocked down, stripped bare, and the only choice we have, short of faith abandonment, is to fling ourselves on the sovereignty of God. We might not be able to see the whys and wherefores, but we must begin to affirm that we believe God does.

Third, as we affirm our desire to be devoted to Him, He will begin to exchange peace for anger. We will begin to believe it is possible to actually live, "Do not let the sun go down while you are still angry" (Ephesians 4:26).

Acting out our anger gives us a feeling of control, and it feels good to be in control. Unfortunately, anger is a psychological black hole. The challenge, then, is to make the conscious choice to be filled with the Spirit instead of filled with anger. How? Ephesians 5:19–21 reminds us of the process. Worship, giving thanks for everything, and getting help from others (submitting) are the steps that enable us to walk away from the chains of anger.

Doubting God or His Goodness

This is a close cousin of anger and, left unhealed, it is the next level down on a slippery staircase. I could be wrong, but my reading and man-watching has led me to believe that many of us hold this view of being a Christian:

Being a Christian assures us of two things. First, it assures us of eternal life in heaven. No problems there. Second, as long as we do our best down here, living by the Bible the best we can, and doing the good things good Christians do, we're pretty much guaranteed a decent family, a decent job, and a decent two- or three-car-garage life. If we're good to God, He will be good to us, and by "good to us" we mean a basically wrinkle-resistant life.

Of course, we may never reflect on how foolish this view is. Would Christians in Bangladesh, or the sub-Sahara, even recognize this as Christian thinking? I have my doubts.

When our kids hand us a major setback, or when tragedy

strikes, our neatly constructed theology begins to get blown apart. Recently in Portland, a car plunged off a bridge and the driver drowned. He lost control of the car when the kitten he had just picked up to bring home got out of its box. He was only eighteen and had just graduated from high school. He was an only child, a Christian, and had wonderful Christian parents. Put yourself in that dad's shoes.

If our minds equate "good Christian living" with "a wonderful life," our theology is in deep trouble.

No, God does not promise us a crisis-free life. In fact, and Scripture shows this repeatedly, *bad things happen to good people.* He does promise us, though, that He will comfort us if we let Him. As we learn to speak our doubt and disappointment to Him, we can begin to believe the Lord's words through Isaiah:

> Fear not, for I have redeemed you; I have summoned you by name; you are mine. When you pass through the waters, I will be with you; and when you pass through the rivers, they will not sweep over you. When you walk through the fire, you will not be burned; the flames will not set you ablaze. For I am the Lord, your God, the Holy One of Israel, your Savior. . . .
>
> Isaiah 43:1–3

Guilt

This is one of the most common feelings of a wounded father. We remember a verse like Proverbs 22:6: "Train a child in the way he should go, and when he is old he will not turn from it."

Also, we reason, "If my kid is mainly a product of his or her upbringing, and now he's so messed up, I must have failed to bring him up properly."

Wounded fathers can have real guilt, that is, feel guilty because they really are, and false guilt, which is feeling guilty when they are not to blame.

Real guilt is the experience of a father who has sinned in the raising of a son or daughter. Sexual, physical, and verbal abuse are all *sins,* and God does not exempt the natural consequences of sin from occurring. A father who is cold, authoritarian, and high in demands will drive his self-esteem-starved kids to their peers. There they will find acceptance. If they get sucked into a negative peer group instead of a positive one, there will be trouble in their lives.

Some men realize too late the error they have made. They have sinned, and their kids are out of control as a result.

What is such a father to do? As with any sin, first confess it to God. According to 1 John 1:9, you know you are forgiven. To your kids, the fact that you have received God's forgiveness makes little difference. If, however, you ask their forgiveness and couple that humble request with an obvious change of behavior, there may be hope for improvement. A once cold and crabby father beginning to show the fruit of the Spirit will be a powerful testimony.

What about *false guilt?* Read the scholars and commentators, and you will see that Proverbs 22:6 is not intended as a promise. It is a statement of the way things usually work but not a "I'm hanging all my self-esteem on this one" promise. Are you offended by this approach to Proverbs? Don't be. Look again at what is really there, and you'll have to agree. For example, do plans always go wrong without counsel and do they always succeed when we get advice? (15:22). Is the house of proud people guaranteed to be torn down? Has there never been a case when a widow's property lines have been violated? (15:25). Yes, these things are generally true, but they are not promises.

Still unsure? Proverbs 22:6 can't be a promise because if it were, our kids would not have free will. They have free will and so do we.

We should not heap false guilt on ourselves for how our kids turn out. Of course, no parent is perfect, and there will always be things we wish we could do over again. Yet wistful regret is one thing; guilt paralysis is quite another.

The son or daughter who has wounded you has a free will, and that free will was installed by God Himself. That's why there is such a party in heaven when the prodigal son returns. It's his choice!

Self-doubt

As adult men, we carefully construct our view of ourselves in the world around us. If our lives could be viewed as a football field, the first fifty yards might be labeled "career," the next twenty yards "husband," the next ten "father," the next ten "deacon/church leader," and so on. Through a typical day and a typical week, we cycle through our various roles, spending time on each section of the playing field.

When a son or daughter hands us an experience that sends us reeling, it's as if a bomb got dropped on that section of the field. No matter where we go on the field, no matter what we are doing, we can easily see the crater, the rubble, and the mess. It affects us wherever we are, whatever we do.

To change the analogy, it's like trying to walk thigh-deep in the surf as the tide is going out. There is a strong undertow. It's hard to walk ahead, and we could easily get pulled under.

Are you feeling the undertow? How can we learn to be strong against it?

A broken-world experience reminds us that we are not ultimately in control. We can't enforce our perfect will. It is hard enough to enforce even our imperfect preferences. We are reminded that it is ultimately God we must trust, not our own strength, wisdom, and skills.

In my research for *Teen Shaping*, I received a stirring letter from a very articulate young lady. Even today, I can hardly read it without getting on my knees to pray for my own three kids and affirm to God that I believe it is only because of Him I have hope as a parent:

"Pray for your kids! Have absolutely no confidence in your good intentions or whatever parental qualifications you may have. My parents are both graduates of a highly respected Bible college. My father has a Ph.D. in the behavioral sciences. Both are committed Christians and walk closely with the Lord. Yet despite these apparently foolproof qualifications, they failed to figure out that their oldest child (me) was taking large and frequent doses of various substances such as LSD, PCP, speed, as well as 'organics.' Perhaps you marvel at my parents' inability to perceive that which should be so obvious; perhaps you marvel at my church's failure to reach out to me as I was being dragged down by the Enemy.

"If so, marvel even more at the shrewdness and frightening precision of Satan's psychological attacks. They (the attacks) are so subtle and sly that we are defeated without even noticing. The battles will take place in the minds of your children, which, despite X years of experience, brilliant education, wondrous qualifications, and your highest hopes, are veritably inaccessible to you. But there is One who has access, and the power to win those battles . . . it is to Him you must make your pleas and entrust your kids."

Concern for My Own Reputation

For better or worse, our reputations are impacted by how well our kids turn out. Come with me to Husky Stadium on game day and seek out the dads of those first-stringers winning down there on the field. See the twinkle in their eyes. See the smiles on their faces as their sons' names become household words to the seventy thousand cheering fans. See also their self-esteem stock soar as, like kings receiving guests, friends pay homage to the fathers of sports-famous sons.

There is nothing wrong, of course, with having a sports-famous son. However, those who have kids who are infamous for evil instead of famous for good really struggle with reputation. God reserves the right to let whatever is propping up their self-esteem get kicked out from under them.

As we learn to grow in our devotion to the Lord (remember chapter 2?), we become more able to say with the Apostle Paul, "For to me, to live is Christ and to die is gain" (Philippians 1:21). "May I never boast except in the cross of our Lord Jesus Christ, through which the world has been crucified to me, and I to the world" (Galatians 6:14).

Blaming

Who is to blame for our sons' or daughters' problems? If it is not altogether our fault, then it must be the partial fault of someone else. We can blame peer pressure, an unloving youth group, Satan, the school system, an incompetent wife, etc., etc., etc.

It is human to try to assess blame. It is divine to be able to let it go. In trying to blame, we are at the same time trying to make ourselves feel better, to justify our actions and our past. In learning to let go of the need to blame, we take a major step in maturity. Instant replaying our own failures and the failures of others doesn't move us any closer to healing and hope. It only delays the process. We are making progress as we finally learn to, "Cast all your anxiety on him because he cares for you" (1 Peter 5:7).

Stress in My Marriage

Their seventeen-year-old daughter Nancy came in an hour later than planned. "Ben was reluctant to talk to Nancy. He felt his wife was being unnecessarily suspicious and that her suspicions would only deepen a rift which had begun to grow between daughter and parents. Ben's policy (if it could be called a policy) was to hope that the division was not serious and that it would heal itself with time. Jean on the other hand felt the rift called for action and that Ben was running away from the problem. So the two quarreled, and quarreled fiercely. . . ."[3]

John White's hard-hitting book continues, "Problems with children have as great a potential to strengthen marriage as to wreck it. They can bring you together in a new unity, or blow you apart."[4]

In my two decades as a youth pastor, I have seen about as many couples nearly destroyed by the rebellion of their kids as I have strengthened by it.

Why do problems with the kids cause marital conflict? Problems get out in the open. The true standards and "default patterns" of the parents become apparent. Example: Some fathers are quite passive and choose to ignore or pass off problems. When pushed, though, they explode unpredictably. Some mothers, by contrast, seek more communication and interaction with the child. This is the difference between Ben and Jean above. Their individual "default patterns" are in direct conflict.

Couples often do not have the resources within themselves to solve these problems. There is too much pride involved, too much blaming or unwillingness to compromise. One of the best steps toward healing is to talk with a trusted pastor or Christian counselor. There is no shame in admitting the need for help.

If possible, get into a men's support group where you can compare notes with other men whose kids are a problem. See how other men are trying to make marriage work under these tough circumstances.

Even if there is stress between you and your wife, fall asleep at night thanking God for her good points. (It wouldn't hurt to tell her these good points too!) Then say with the Psalmist, "Be at rest once more, O my soul, for the Lord has been good to you" (Psalm 116:7).

The Rebirth of Hope

It wasn't the failure of a son or daughter that caused Pastor Gordon MacDonald to have a broken-world experience. It was his own moral failure that caused his life and ministry to crash around him. Through the dust and ashes, however, God worked and reworked in MacDonald's life and heart. When our world breaks apart, he affirms, God can do some amazing things in our lives. His book *Rebuilding Your Broken World* is a series of "bottom lines," and here are three most appropriate for hurting fathers:

"Bottom Line #13: The freest person in the world is one with an open heart, a broken spirit, and a new direction in which to travel.

"Bottom Line #14: The process of rebuilding requires some temporary operating principles by which to navigate through dark times.

"Bottom Line #15: Listen; receive; give; then anticipate. No time in the wilderness is ever wasted for the one who intends to return what grace has given."[5]

Wounded fathers, hurting fathers; a high tide of human pain is awash in our country. Receive strength from the One who made you, and with perhaps a longing sigh pray with Job, "I know that my Redeemer lives, and that in the end he will stand upon the earth. And after my skin has been destroyed, yet in my flesh I will see God" (Job 19:25, 26).

Questions for Discussion

1. Are you a wounded father? From the survey on pages 174 and 175, share the items in which you circled a 4 or a 5.

2. Review each of the Scripture verses listed in the seven characteristics of a wounded father. Which of these means the most to you now, and why?

3. Which of Gordon MacDonald's three principles do you find most encouraging? Why?

Idea Corner 10

With Preschoolers

Remember Play-Doh? Just like bubbles, the technology and ancillary equipment options for this play medium have exploded over the years. Visit the Play-Doh section of a large toy store and prepare to be amazed. Festooned or not with extra equipment, Play-Doh plus child plus dad equal the right ingredients for a batch of fun.

With Elementary Age

Pet photography can be a fun and profitable enterprise for dad and son or daughter. Fully automatic 35mm cameras are not hard to use and have come way down in price. Take some sample pictures of your own pets and get some picture folders at your local photography supply store. Make your samples even more fun with "stick on" captions, also available at many photography stores. Next step, take your show on the road. Go to friends or just door-to-door and offer to take pictures of pets and people (for a small fee, of course).

Print a nice brochure, get a business card and business license, learn a few tricks of the trade, and this hobby can earn your kid a good income.

With Teenagers

Many high schools no longer require physical education. Decide with your son or daughter that you will stay in shape together. Hold yourselves accountable for eating right. Decide on a regular form of exercise that you can do together: running, tennis, swimming, racquetball, using fitness-center equipment. Decide what you'll do and how often you'll do it. You will be surprised at how much good communication can result as you do this activity together.

The Renewed Father

Through the dim morning light filtering into the room, I could see something at the breakfast table my sleepy eyes didn't recognize. No, it wasn't a gray egg. It was construction paper cut in the shape of a heart. A smiling sunshine face filled half the heart. On the other half, these words were written:

TO DAD:
A dad who loves and a dad who cares
A dad who's braver than twenty-one bears
For a dad who I love and a dad who loves me
For a dad who's funny and a dad who is stern
A dad whose the best in the whole wide world.
. . .You are my only sunshine.
Love,
MaryAnn

Wow. We're not into fathering to get thanks like this, but it sure feels great when it comes. It gave me a boost that day, no doubt about it! It made me want to be an even better father.

Do all dads want to enjoy their kids more and learn to be better? Unfortunately, no. Burnout is a problem for parents. For fathers to keep from being burned out, we need to keep ourselves constantly renewed. If we don't, we can stumble down a staircase of disillusionment and despair. Here is what happens to some dads:

Step 1: Initial enthusiasm and high hopes about being a dad.

Step 2: Initial clash of idealism versus reality: being a dad is *work*.

Step 3: Frustration when experience of fathering doesn't meet expectation. Attempts to fix what is wrong.

Step 4: Severe frustration when efforts to fix things don't work.

Step 5: The father "gives up" fathering. He may stay in the marriage but doesn't like his kids or try to relate to them. His motivation to be a better dad becomes zero.

We make choices at Step 3 or Step 4 that either help us pull out of this descent or propel us down toward burnout.

My friend at church who told me, "Raising teenagers is a miserable experience," was putting his first foot on the fifth and final step down. He has planted both feet there now. He is sullen, angry, and has turned over all parenting decisions to his wife. His kids hear from him only when they have done something wrong, and then he yells.

We try to put on the Band-Aids of eating, alcohol, or expensive adult toys to make up for our disenchantment with fathering. Burned-out fathers hurt marriages. Burned-out fathers hurt kids. Burned-out fathers are of little use to God.

With the stakes so high, let's look at ten ideas that will help us keep off that slippery staircase and instead stay renewed while learning to be good dads.

The Renewed Father Survey

	Generally No	50/50	Generally Yes
1. I have pretty good control of my time and do not feel I'm out of control.	___	___	___
2. My marriage is going well.	___	___	___
3. I have hobbies or interests outside my career and take time to enjoy them.	___	___	___
4. My kids and I do things together that we really enjoy.	___	___	___
5. I am in a support group or Bible study where I can be honest about my struggles and held accountable.	___	___	___
6. I get regular exercise and am physically fit.	___	___	___

	Generally No	50/50	Generally Yes
7. I get ideas about learning to be a better father from other men, books, and other resources.	_____	_____	_____
8. I try to keep failure and problems in proper perspective, realizing that God is bigger than any and all my problems.	_____	_____	_____
9. I am able to revise my expectations if I realize they are unrealistic.	_____	_____	_____
10. I am growing spiritually in my devotion to God.	_____	_____	_____

Scoring: 3 for every "Generally No"
2 for every "50/50"
1 for every "Generally Yes"

22+ You are burned out or almost there. Immediate improvement essential.

18-22 Borderline. Danger ahead if no changes made.

14-17 Pretty good but still room for improvement.

10-13 Excellent, keep it up!

If you aren't too happy about your score, don't start heaping
guilt on yourself. Okay, things need improvement, but don't
think that, after reading this chapter, you'll go out there gung ho
and be the ultimate renewed father. No, decide now to choose
only two areas to improve on in the next two months. Once you
see real progress in these two areas, tackle another two. Let's
look at each area now, with honest minds and open hearts.

Time

I know a man who is going to have better control of his time,
someday soon. He is a doctor and is very much in demand. He
loves his two kids and they enjoy him on the rare occasions he
is home. Yep, he's going to get better at time management and
be a much better father, husband, and dedicated Christian layman . . . someday.

He has been saying this for the last twelve years. Just a few
more years, and both his kids will be out of high school. Will he
ever change? I'm not holding my breath.

We have already talked a lot about time in chapter 6. It is one
of the main problems today's men face. Here are some practical
ideas to get a grip.

Know how you use your time now. How many hours a week do
you work? Write it on a calendar with the rest of your normal
activities, including your devotional life.

Step back and evaluate. Is this a balanced life? Do you really
have control of where your time goes? If not, what can you do to
get more control? I strongly believe that, the more hours a man
works at a job each week, *the better he has to manage his nonwork-
ing time.*

As a pastor, my work week normally runs fifty to fifty-five
hours, occasionally much more. I use a system, however, that
lets my family know I am giving them high priority. Not every

week is the same, but there is a basic pattern to my "off time." Curious? Here is when I am normally off and what generally happens to that time:

Monday night
  fun stuff with kids/available to help with homework
  money management
Tuesday night (home twice a month)
  personal projects
  time with kids
Thursday (my day off)
  Morning: home fix-up and repair, projects with my wife
  Afternoon: relaxation, personal projects
  Evening (home twice a month):
  mainly time with my wife
Friday night
  family fun night
Saturday afternoon
  family fun or dad/kid one-on-one time
  personal projects

I run three times a week in the early morning and have devotions in the morning as well. The above schedule doesn't always work out exactly as listed, but it's the basic plan. We all seem to function pretty well using this system. Where does TV fit in to this? I watch the national news while doing the dishes. Beyond that, about two hours a week is my average. My wife doesn't watch TV at all, except for the news.

Our kids and TV? *See* Idea Corner 11.

Write your plan, and share it with your spouse. Try it for a few weeks and see how everyone feels. Change as needed.

Marriage

A healthy marriage is a prerequisite for being a renewed father. If there are major cracks in the marriage foundation, emotional energy will drain through those cracks, and there will be none left for the kids.

Of course, books abound on how to keep a marriage working. Unfortunately I've seen many marriages break up, and the pattern becomes sadly routine. Unbeknown to anyone, one of the marriage partners becomes unhappy. He or she does not share that unhappiness with the spouse. The unhappiness, stemming from an unmet need or other problem, continues. On the surface, all may seem well. The hurting partner may hint at a problem but never confronts it directly.

As the months (or years) go by, the seriousness of the problem in the mind of the hurting spouse grows. The problem looms so large that the hurting partner begins to envision life without the spouse. He or she begins to rebuild a mental picture of being single or being in love with someone else. At some point, this mental scenario becomes not just a theoretical possibility but a goal.

When this line is crossed, what I call the "let's gather evidence" stage begins. The hurting partner accumulates mental documentation of other failures and shortcomings of the spouse. These "crimes" mount, providing inner assurance that the already-made choice to uncouple was right, logical, and moral.

When enough evidence is garnered, the final-preparation phase begins. The hurting partner begins to rehearse the announcement of doom as well as make concrete plans for being single. Once everything is ready, rehearsed, and planned to the smallest details, it is time for "the announcement."[1]

Kent came home from a hard day at the office. As he pulled into the driveway, he wondered where the Volvo was. Usually his wife was home with their two preschoolers. He opened the kitchen door and headed, as he always did, to where the day's mail lay. It was there, as usual, but there was also a note from Pam: "Kent, you are my enemy and my oppressor. I cannot live with you or be married to you any longer. You should have seen this coming but did not, of course. It's too late now. You will hear from my attorney in the next couple of days."

Kent didn't even know his wife was unhappy! You may think this is fiction, but it is not. I have personally seen three marriages end just this dramatically, and each husband was clueless until his wife dropped the big bomb.

I am not a marriage counselor, but based on what I have seen and experienced, I offer five practical suggestions.

First, schedule time to stay in touch. Our wives need to know we want to listen to them. Often, at the end of a wild day at the office, we men are all talked out. We have heard and said all we can handle. Our wives, on the other hand, may not have had that kind of day at their jobs or at home. They have been saving things they want to talk about. If we forever act disinterested in listening to what our wives want to say, or are just too busy, our marriages are in serious, serious trouble. If, on the other hand, we create a climate where they can share their feelings, we are much more apt to be able to deal with their hurts before they decide we have become "enemies and oppressors."

Second, make time to have fun. Shared activities, whether yard work or racquetball, make for continued enjoyment of the relationship.

Third, don't put off the repair projects your wife wants done around the house. It may not be frustrating to you that the Dutch door is broken, but your wife hears it creak every time little Johnny races through.

Fourth, remember to say words of kindness, affirmation, and appreciation every single day.

Fifth, pray together daily, and share your own spiritual journeys.

I can't guarantee a glassy, calm, Love Boat relationship, but I do know that these five things can't do anything but help a marriage work.

A marriage that is healthy makes it possible to feel encouraged, renewed, and supported as a dad.

Other Interests

Some jobs or careers don't just require our minds but our hearts and souls as well. A major software company in Seattle is being sued by a former employee. He alleges he was fired because he was married and had "outside interests." This company, it is alleged, wants all its employees to be single or have a single life-style, work fifty hours a week or more, and attend frequent seminars and company social gatherings. Employees should eat, sleep, breathe, and live the company.[2]

There is nothing wrong with being devoted to a career, but it is so easy to get consumed by it that you have no time for or interest in anything else. If only one activity, your job, arouses your adrenaline, you are going to be pretty dull to your spouse and kids.

Learning new skills keeps us young and refreshed. I know a pastor who has become a race car driver. Think of the sermon illustrations he's going to reap from that! I know a respected dentist who is an avid world traveler. The slides this man has of seemingly everywhere and everything are truly mind-boggling. I recently attended my daughter's piano recital. All the students of her teacher performed, including a man who was thirty-eight. He's been at it for two years now. Though he stumbled his way through a piece my daughter knew when she was nine, I couldn't help but admire his willingness to learn a new skill.

Perhaps you have so many outside interests and hobbies that you find work and family interfere with your enjoyment of them. Understand that some men face the opposite challenge. They need to learn to diversify, which brings us to the next area.

Doing Things You Enjoy With Your Kids

Question: When you were a kid, would you have chosen an adult like you for a friend? You can see what I'm getting at. As your kids grow, they will choose for friends peers who have similar interests. They will be drawn to adults who have similar interests as well. For fathers, the message is clear: mutual enjoyment of activities builds relationships. There is a big bonus in this as well: such activities refresh us instead of draining us.

I hate playing house, but I love to build houses. Being blessed with three daughters means I was asked a zillion times when the girls were young to join them in playing house. I agreed many times, but to call the enjoyment mutual would definitely be redefining the word *mutual*. I never came away from playing house feeling refreshed, just drained.

Get out the LEGO bricks, though, and I woke up! We built some amazing homes and other buildings, and I came away feeling great.

Yes, I read my share of stories to the kids, and I nearly fell asleep so many times that my girls would have to correct my slurred speech as my eyelids seemed lead-heavy. No one had to rouse me out of semislumber, though, when we played with the electric train or race car set.

Now that they are teenagers, we enjoy bike riding, running, tennis, football, hiking, washing the car, and all sorts of activities. When I do these things, I'm refreshed. Put me in a fabric store for ten minutes, though, and my eyelids again are made of lead.

Support Group

In chapter 2, we saw involvement in a support or account-ability group as essential to growth in our devotion to God. It is important to stay renewed as fathers as well. We need an environment in which we can be honest and vulnerable with the problems we feel and the wounds we bare.

Joining a group isn't magic. It takes awhile to learn to trust. Once we can trust, the potential for our refreshment is almost limitless. I'm in a group that meets twice a month. Often as I drive to the meeting, I'm thinking about how tired I am and how else I could or should be using the time. When I leave, though, I'm so grateful for the experience and the renewal that comes when one can be honest with people and be honestly supported.

Physically Fit

Many of my friends have forsaken their sedentary ways, lost some weight, and become physically fit. To a man they have said, "I feel so much better," or, "I have so much more energy." It's true.

Options abound: fast-walking, running, biking, skating, swimming, and a multitude of others. When we are out there doing our exercise thing, it helps us work out the stress. Sometimes when I run I feel as if I'm working through my stress in a very tangible way.

I've been a runner since grad school days and, Lord willing, I'll be a runner until I die. I combine running with prayer. On my normal route, which I do three mornings a week, I enjoy a great time with God. I run more often if I'm training for a race, and then I bring verses of Scripture on small cards to think and pray about en route. My goal is to be capable of a respectable half marathon (thirteen miles) throughout the year.

Running doesn't exercise everything, though. I have found

that forty push-ups and forty sit-ups three or four mornings a week keep my front and back muscles in pretty good condition. I hate push-ups, but I do them to keep in shape, not for fun.

Do you love to eat? I do. My wife has done graduate work in nutrition and has helped me see the light about food. Some people, it seems, live to eat. I, by God's grace, eat to live. She has instructed me carefully on the fat content of various foods. I know that if more than 20 percent of my calories come from fat in any given day, I am layering sludge in my arteries. I also know that if it is down to 10 percent, some of the previous sludge gets cleaned out.

So, I watch fat. I can handle a maple bar in the morning at the office if my lunch is going to be fruit and rice cakes. On the other hand, one cheeseburger-fries-shake lunch puts me over 20 percent for the whole day. So does pizza. So do a lot of other things I dearly enjoy eating. I'll confess I reach my "percentage fat content" goal only three or four days a week, but that's better than a few years ago.

Fathering Resources

When I teach youth ministry seminars, one of my favorite sayings is this: "To stay fresh in youth ministry, you need to steal like a bandit." Most youth workers are not very creative, but they are good adapters of what they see other youth workers do.

I believe the same about fathering. Most of us don't come up with father-improvement ideas on our own. We can, however, adapt what we see others doing.

We can get help in learning to be better dads by first watching other fathers we respect. This is just the beginning, however. There is a plethora of fathering resources now available. Books, both secular and Christian, abound. (You're reading one of them!) There are video resources aimed at dads, and most Christian bookstores now carry a line of videos for rental. Magazines, both secular and Christian, can be helpful. Encourage your church to hold seminars of interest to fathers or even host a "Dad's University" (*see* chapter 13).

In the business world, the importance of continuing education and sharpening skills is assumed. In something so important as being a dad, continuing education should be a high priority as well.

Perspective on Problems

A dad recently confided to me, "We may have had a setback on that issue, but he's a good kid and we're keeping communication lines open." He has a strong-willed son who doesn't consider it "cool" to attend church. This dad could see his coercion attempts were backfiring, so he simply redefined his goals. Yes, he deeply wants his son to attend church, but he has decided not to let this setback make his whole attitude about parenting this boy go down the drain.

No matter what happens when we father, God is still God. Jesus Christ is still our Savior. When He comes, all wrongs will be righted. Our rightness will be vindicated. In the meantime, we have His comfort and His peace, as we grow in devotion to Him.

I consider that our present sufferings are not worth comparing with the glory that will be revealed in us. The creation waits in eager expectation for the sons of God to be revealed. . . . We know that the whole creation has been groaning as in the pains of childbirth right up to the present time. Not only so, but we ourselves, who have the firstfruits of the Spirit, groan inwardly as we wait eagerly for our adoption as sons, the redemption of our bodies.

Romans 8:18–23

The angst we may feel as fathers is part and parcel of our participation in a less-than-perfect world. We have, as Christians, much better days to look forward to. This viewpoint of remembering the eternal can refresh and renew us when things go bad.

Flexibility

A cousin of the previous area, this skill helps us adapt to the changing needs of our kids. Some fathers have unrealistic expectations for their kids and for the experience of being a parent. If we learn how to be flexible as our kids get older, the resulting reduction of stress will help keep us renewed.

I was quite shocked by several findings in my survey of four hundred Christian families for the book *Teen Shaping*. The heavy-handed/authoritarian approach to discipline was still used with seventeen- to nineteen-year-olds in 10 percent of the homes.[3] It was no surprise, however, that this approach was unsuccessful two-thirds of the time with kids that age.[4]

A good example of how flexibility reduces stress is Mike Yaconelli, founder of Youth Specialties, whom we met back in chapter 5. Despite everything he and his wife could dream up, one of his sons was getting average grades in high school. Finally, he ceased to make it an issue and accepted him as he was. Stress reduction naturally resulted. His attitude about church attendance for his "pastor's kids" teenagers reveals flexibility too. Yes, they will normally come to church, but if they are too tired every now and then, he lets them sleep and doesn't make an issue of it.

Flexibility can reduce our fathering stress and help keep us renewed in the process.

Spiritual Growth

Devotion to God with as much gusto as most of us men are devoted to sports . . . we laid this foundation many pages ago and have come back to it many times since. Our life in Christ is the ultimate source of the renewal we experience as men and as fathers. Stop growing spiritually and stop living a life with the Lord as our best Friend, and our inner emotional reserves can rapidly get sucked dry by the pressures and problems of parenting.

These ten ideas can help us keep renewed as fathers. Individually or in combination, they will help recharge our emotional batteries so we can be good dads. If we are going to reach anything close to peak performance in parenting, we must learn to use our emotional energy wisely and restore it wisely as well.[5]

Don't take these ten ideas and charge ahead trying to become the ultimate good example in all of them. Instead, take two. Pray and focus on them in the next couple of months. Share your decision with your spouse. When you feel as if progress has been made, begin work on two more. These are realistic steps in learning to be renewed as a father.

Speaking of your spouse, she plays a pivotal role in your success as a husband and father. Have her read the next chapter too.

Questions for Discussion

1.   What was your score on The Renewed Father Survey? How do you feel about that?

2.   Do you know any marriages that have fallen apart in the way described in this chapter? Explain.

3.   Which two of the ten areas will you try to improve in the next two months? How will you know when you have made progress in these areas?

4.   Open your Bible to Psalm 116:1–9. Which of these verses

do you find most true or most encouraging as you seek to
be a renewed father?

Idea Corner 11

With Preschoolers

Do you mind looking a little weird for a while? Your preschoolers, both boys and girls, will enjoy doing a make-over of
dad. Supply them with lipstick, hair gel, powder, and whatever
else your wife can donate to the cause. Have a camera or camcorder handy, because this is an experience you'll want to enjoy
again and again.

With Elementary Age

Both boys and girls this age enjoy the challenge and responsibility of baking cookies. Choose your best chocolate chip cookie
recipe and make a huge batch. Box them nicely and take them
to your local fire department as a thank-you for service to the
community.

Elementary-age kids can easily be addicted to TV. Negotiate a
weekly TV watching limit. (It's five hours at the Kageler house.)
Make tokens or coupons out of construction paper (use a different color for each kid) and label each with a different number:
"30 Minutes," "15 Minutes," "10 Minutes," and "5 Minutes"—
enough for five hours total time. Put a container with all the
tokens and a "spent" box on the TV. Whenever the kids watch
TV, they take an appropriate token and place it in the "spent"
box. When they are out of tokens, their TV time is over for the
week. On Monday morning, all the "spent" tokens are put back
in the container on the TV, and another week begins.

With Teenagers

What is of major interest to your teenager? Sports? Music? Hollywood? Art? Politics? Business? Pick a field of interest, and go on a hunt for Christians. Your pastor or youth pastor may have a file of organizations (Fellowship of Christian Athletes, for example) that minister or represent Christians in this field of interest. Young people have heroes. They look up to people who have proven competence in areas they find appealing. It will encourage them (and you) to discover strong and unapologetic Christians in these fields.

Part IV

Outside Help

How a Wife Can Help Her Husband Be a Better Dad

I always forget to have a box of tissues in my office until it's too late. Mary didn't waste any time with small talk and pleasantries. She sat down and started. She cried, I listened.

In between sobs and silence, I heard a familiar but tragic story of insensitivity, heavy-handedness, anger, and emotional neglect. The children hated him. She, well . . . she still cared but her ability to live with this beast/man was fading fast. They were both well-respected members of the congregation. To others, they seemed an ideal Christian couple, with wonderful Christian children. Getting weary of living a lie, she wondered, *Should I take the kids and run?* Her coming to my office was a last gasp for hope. How could she help this man become a decent husband and dad?

This chapter is addressed to wives. I hope your situation has not reached the point where you are rehearsing your divorce announcement or plotting the when and how of becoming a single parent. You may be hurting so much you want to scream.

On the other hand, you may only want to help encourage your already fine husband in his role as father. Let me speak to you. The fact that you are reading this says you feel a need at some level. You want to see your husband improve in some way as a dad. I'll try to answer three questions:

1. What can I do if we are expecting our first child or if that child is less than a year old?
2. What can I do if our kids are older?
3. What do I do is my husband seems unwilling to change at all?

One Man and a Baby

If you are normal, you've been pondering being a mom for years. Even in high school, the thought crossed your mind many times. After high school until today, whenever you saw a cute baby in a stroller, you felt something tug within you. It's as if you were born to be a mom.

Please realize that your husband had no such thoughts in high school. As for cute babies in strollers . . . what cute babies? He didn't even see them. (*Cute babes*, yes, he saw them all right, but that's another story.) He wasn't born to be a dad as you were born to be a mother. He was born to compete, make money, provide, and climb.[1] Your husband is confronting fatherhood and babydom for the first time in his life, and honestly, it scares him a lot.

Frankly, one of the things that makes him feel even more insecure is you. You seem so happy, excited, and worst of all, competent. You are ready, and he can tell that all this baby business is coming from somewhere deep down inside you. He's seeing a side of you that was only theory before. Yes, he is interested in this baby and has a nervous happiness about what has happened. He may feel happy, but you can bet your last

Pamper that he doesn't feel competent. This disparity of perceived competence causes some men to hang back and not get involved with their infant children.

You, mom, can change that.

According to Martin Greenberg, who has studied these things enough to be an expert, you need to do two things with this nervous/hanging-back dad: (1) give him permission to participate with the baby and (2) give him the space to actually do it.[2] You give permission by verbally saying, "Come on, dear, give me a hand with the bath," or, "Wow, I'm really beat. Could you give the bottle this evening?" It may seem too simple, but some men never offer to help because they are so intimidated by your expert competence.

How can you give him space? Sometimes you give him space by getting sick or going back to work. Then he has to get involved and take responsibility, or some of the job just won't get done. But short of these, you give your husband space by asking him to give the bath or change the diaper and then getting far enough away so you can't be easily consulted. On a Saturday afternoon, give yourself a break and go to the mall or out for a few sets of tennis with a friend. Let your husband be in charge of the kid for a few hours. His competence and confidence will build as he realizes the baby isn't going to fall apart when you leave.

Support and encourage him as a dad. When the baby smiles at him, make a big deal about it. Compliment him on his irresistible personality. (You married him, right?) If the wailing starts when he holds the baby, don't criticize, read him the riot act, or take the baby back into your competent motherly embrace. Affirm him and let him know that nasty kid cries for you too, and you feel pretty stupid when it happens.

Your attitude is so important here. A few words of sarcasm or some well-placed put-downs will slam doors of communication.

You may feel like the victor, you may feel as if you are the one with the power in this relationship, but your berating will turn him away from the baby now and reduce the potential for good communication later.

If you are beyond the baby stage and you realize in reading this that you were a nagging and critical young mother, it might not hurt to bring this up with your husband and apologize. And what if he won't apologize for his jerklike behavior to you? Leave that to God and him. Your taking the initiative to restore and heal the relationship may break the communication gridlock between yourself and your husband as well as your husband and child.

Beyond Babyhood

If your kids are beyond infancy, there are at least four things you can do to help your husband learn to be a better dad. You may not see yourself moving in all four of these areas at once, but do what you can.

Taming the Tongue

It is as important when the kids are older as when they are younger: don't nag, scold, or verbally clobber your spouse about his fathering, or anything else, for that matter. Yes, I know, the male ego is famous (or infamous) among women. Yes, I know it is galling that men respond to female adulation. Like it or not, words of kindness and affirmation are much more effective than criticism.

Picture this: It's Sunday morning. Only heaven knows why, but you agreed to be the Sunday-school teacher for the four-year-olds. You should be in the classroom by 9:15 A.M. Your family lives fifteen minutes from church, and it's now 8:59 A.M. You have delegated to Jerry, your husband, the simple task of dressing Tosha, your three-year-old girl, while you make sure your nine-

and eleven-year-olds have their act together. *Click.* It's now 9:00 A.M. Jerry and Tosha emerge from the bedroom all smiles. Jerry looks proud, and Tosha is her usual smiling self. In less than a second, the horrible truth registers deep inside your brain. Tosha's dress is on backwards, her socks don't match, and her hair looks like rats have been playing soccer in it all night.

Your reaction would be:

A. "Jerry, you jerk. Look what you've done! She looks as if she's been dressed by a committee of gorillas. I can't trust you with the simplest task, can I? Call the church and tell Mary we're going to be late . . . I don't know how long it's going to take me to undo this mess!"

B. "Jerry, well, this is certainly going to be a memorable morning. Quick, grab the camera. I appreciate your efforts and I see you both look pretty proud. I'm proud too. The people at church are going to love this one. Let's go."

Jerry may have the competence of a slug when it comes to fashion, but criticism and put-downs won't help. Affirmation, humor, and encouragement will. If you had chosen B, after church you would have had the possibility of doing a little seminar for Jerry and Tosha about matching socks, the directionality of dresses, and other topics of high fashion.

Still not convinced that kind words are better than frying-pan words? How do *you* like to be spoken to when you've done something less-than-perfect?

I rest my case.

Delegating Discipline

Men fall into two extremes here.

Some men exercise a virtual reign of terror in the home. With incredible gusto, they mete out discipline and punishment, convinced they are the instruments of the wrath of God. If your husband is like that, skip to "Talking With a Tree Trunk" on page 214.

Other men, and it is these we will talk about here, abdicate discipline to you, the mother. After all, you are with the kids more. You see their mistakes, and you are right there to take care of the discipline.

There is one big problem with this approach: boys respect discipline from the father much more than they do from the mother. The father has to be highly involved in discipline, especially if the son is strong-willed.

You and your husband need to agree that discipline is just one of the ways we teach as parents, and that if it is done properly our kids can reap tremendous benefits. Affirm your husband with the words, "I see you as our main provider and protector. I believe you can be the best guider of the children when they make mistakes. I know they will respect your discipline because I know they love you so much."

This whole idea was heavy on my heart in the writing of *Teen Shaping: Solving the Discipline Dilemma*. Eighteen different discipline methods are discussed. Some are better to use at different ages and with different personality types. Of these eighteen, there are some that fulfill three important positive discipline criteria: building self-esteem, building responsibility, and building the family as a Christian support group. With a little training, a man can excel when it comes to providing the positive discipline sons and daughters need.

One-on-One

Encourage your husband to spend one-on-one time with the kids. Realize he is probably not geared that way automatically. He feels comfortable in the adult world, facing adult problems and dealing with life in adult ways. The mind of a five-year-old is probably a mystery to him, so he won't automatically want to do this.

Encourage it anyway. Set the example by taking your daughter to breakfast monthly, just you and her. Encourage him to take the boy out regularly, "man-to-man." This will mean so much to your son, he'll never forget it.

Encourage his one-on-one time with your daughter too. I know a teenage girl who is really struggling with her feelings about her father. She loves him, but he obviously enjoys her brothers more than her. As a teenager, she is behaving exactly like other girls who are starved for affection and approval from their fathers. Since she can't get it from him, she is boy crazy. She is hungry for male attention. Her dad won't give it to her, and she is discovering her sexuality is appealing to boys.

If your husband still is not prone to do one-on-one things, try a different twist. Does a friend of your spouse have a daughter or son the same age as yours? Suggest that your husband and your friend take the girls or boys out for dessert, a baseball game, bowling, fishing, anything. The two children will see this as a special time, and it will be appreciated.

In Touch With Resources

"Jim, I heard they're showing Dobson's films series *Turn Your Heart Toward Home* at Jon and Sara's church. Remember how they both raved about it? Let's give it a try. I know there are ways I want to improve as a parent."

This wife made her pitch very wisely. She did *not* say, "Jim, you turkey, I think you need to be a better father, so why don't you go to these Dobson films, and maybe they can help you get straightened up."

Obviously, the wrong approach.

You want to be a better mother too, right? When you hear of parenting seminars or parenting film series, suggest you go together. Affirm your own need to improve. Ask for your husband's support. When you attend, he will get some input and help as well, and you will both benefit.

Find a good book on parenting. Read it through together, talking about each chapter. Tell him *you* need this help, and you value his input as you read along.

I sincerely hope at least some of the above sounds practical. But what if it doesn't? What if you are living with a man who does not recognize his need to change and rebuffs any attempt on your part to help him see the light?

Talking With a Tree Trunk

Remember when it was in vogue to talk to your houseplants? Speaking kindly to them, in warm and reassuring tones, would create an ambiance conducive to good growth. At least that was the general idea. I'll confess to having had a few words with our plants, never with much seriousness, however. What I recall being the most frustrating was that I could never get the feeling they were actually listening.

Have you tried to talk to your husband about being a better dad and found it frustrating? Was it kind of like talking with a tree trunk, a cement sidewalk, or a boulder? Some women feel the same way you do. They have tried to get their husbands to see that change is necessary. Their hearts break when they sense the tension escalating between dad and kids.

Let me suggest several possible action steps if you are dealing with a tree-trunk husband.

Prayer

This is obvious in one way but in another way it isn't. Okay, so your husband needs to change. Yes, pray specifically about the behavior that needs changing, but pray something else too. Pray that the Lord will help you see where *you* need to change. Is there an area of your life that is frustrating to your husband? Have you stubbornly resisted any change in your own behavior? If so, God working in your changed life may make your husband much more open to change on his own.

Also, realize that God doesn't guarantee you a husband who will meet your needs and the needs of the kids. But He does promise to meet needs. If you can let go of your "right" to have a husband who is a better father, it frees you to expectantly anticipate how God is going to supply. Please do not take this as an encouragement or justification for marital unfaithfulness! I just know I've seen some hurting women have their attitudes totally changed when they gave over to God their "rights." Funny thing, when their attitudes changed, so did their husbands.

Understanding the Background

When you married your husband, you knew and loved him, yet you didn't know all you do now. In chapter 6, I tried to help fathers realize some of the things blocking their improvement as dads, and it would be helpful for you to take a moment and consider this as well. In the following list, rate each entry on a 0–5 scale. A 5 means, "Yes, this is why he's not a good father," while 0 means, "Does not apply in any way."

_____ His own father was a terrible example.

_____ He was not raised to be caring or nurturing; it was never praised or encouraged.

_____ Early on, because of your supercompetence as a parent, he mentally checked out and has left it all to you.

_____ He just doesn't like the kids and the way they behave.

_____ He sees his main role as breadwinner. That is his contribution to the family.

_____ He is in such a rat race with his job that he has no energy or ability left to give any thought to improving as a dad.

If you have an understanding of why your husband isn't a good dad, you can pray about it more specifically. You can also try other measures to facilitate change.

Specific Steps

Was his father a terrible example? See if you can connect him with a man who is a great example. As you think about the fathers in your church, are there good ones your own husband enjoys (or could enjoy) being around? Invite the couple over for dessert, or go out to dinner—something to get the four of you together. You might even want to speak to the wife of that man first, expressing your dilemma and soliciting their help.

Did your husband receive no reward for nurturing behavior? This is a hard one. First of all, make sure you thank him and express appreciation for any nurturing behavior you see in him. Getting him connected with a good modeler of nurture, as we just discussed, might also be feasible.

Perhaps it is your fault. No, you didn't purposely try to put down his first feeble attempts at parenting, but now you realize that is what you did. Go to him, confess your error of years ago, and ask him to try again, expressing confidence in his abilities.

Your husband just can't stand how the kids behave? Let me ask you this: Truthfully, can you stand how the kids behave? Yes, you're geared to stick up for them, and you realize better than he does that kids must be kids. But are you put out and put off by their behavior too? If so, let him know. Don't criticize your kids in front of them, but help your husband see you are on his side and you are really frustrated. If he sees you are sincere, it might open the door to his willingness to help things change for the better for both of you.

Is he only the breadwinner? If you have any positive communication doors left open with your husband, let him know you are hurting. Don't blame him, don't put him down, just tell him the kids are driving you mad and it would mean so much to you if he would become more involved.

No time due to the rat race? If he is open with you about the stressful treadmill he feels he is on, try to creatively find some more time for him. Example: Does he usually mow the lawn or shovel the snow? See if there is money to have someone else do the grunt work. Say no to the temptation for higher car payments or credit-card debt for the latest this or that. Instead, use that money to pay a responsible kid to do some work for you. This will free the dad's time at least a little bit to be more involved with the children.

For any one or combination of the above situations, it would not hurt to book some time with a good Christian counselor. He or she will have additional suggestions and resources to help you face this seemingly impossible husband/father.

Questions for Discussion

1. How open are you to input from your wife? If or when she does try to suggest appropriate change, how does she do it? How do you respond? Why do you respond the way you do?

2. What is one way your wife could encourage you in your role as a father? Have you told her this?

3. What is one area in which you and your wife are in

agreement about raising the kids? What is one area in which you do not agree?

4. Open your Bible to Psalm 16. Read verses 1, 2, 5, 6, 7, 8, and 11. Which of these can you most identify with today?

Idea Corner 12

With Preschoolers

Every town has a place that sells appliances. Come home with a refrigerator or stove box. Reassemble it using duct tape and behold, this celluloid rectangle can become a succession of creations: a house . . . car . . . ship . . . airplane . . . spacecraft . . . fort . . . jack-in-the-box . . . palace . . . submarine. Write these options on pieces of paper, and each day for ten days, have your child pick a different one. Once the identity of the box has been announced for the day, plunge into your imagination. If you cut out portholes or windows, save the cutouts so you can tape them back in, if necessary, for the next night.

With Elementary Age

Your kids like to watch TV, right? Help them understand what commercial messages are really saying. As soon as a commercial comes on, see who can identify the product first. What is the feeling the commercial says you will have when you have this thing? Is that really true? Play this game for a few weeks, and your kids will begin to automatically critique commercial messages.

With Teenagers

Agree with your teenagers to make a mental note each time either of you laughs uproariously. At suppertime, share your laughing experiences of the day. Try to tell them with enough detail so others in the family can really feel the humor with you.

How the Church Can Help a Man Be a Better Father

The evangelical church in America is waking up to this fact: Men's ministries can be a dynamic and vital part of the church as well as an excellent source of church growth. Some churches make specific mention of fathering only in June and ignore the topic the rest of the year. Some churches find the traditional men's group has become about as popular as cold soup. Get men excited to come to a men's meeting? Ever tried to push a rope?

I don't have statistics about the percentage of churches with vital men's ministries compared with ten years ago. What I see, though, are more and more churches taking men's ministries seriously. Why? There are two reasons, two sides of the same coin, actually, and if you are a pastor, a Christian education director, or a concerned layman in your church, these two reasons ought to make you sit bolt upright and listen.

Reason number one: Most fathers in your church are baby boomers (born 1946–1966). Researchers all over North America are documenting that the majority of these men see their families, and being fathers, as an extremely high priority. They feel all the stress and pressure we've talked about. Offer something that meets their needs, and they'll show up. One church in Seattle offered a men's seminar and expected a few hundred to come. Were they ever surprised when 650 men registered!

Reason number two: Men's ministries can make your church grow! You see, it's not just Christian men who feel stressed out about being fathers; non-Christian men do too. Offer something appealing, market it wisely, have your men bring their friends, and you'll see results.

As you frame your own program, using the ideas and resources listed here and others you can think of, remember two additional insights:

First, baby boomers are not afraid of small groups. They see the value in vulnerability and accountability. Many baby-boomer men, for example, can really get into the questions I've asked at the end of these chapters. On the other hand, fathers born before 1946 may be much less inclined to pull back the shades of their souls and allow others to look in.

Second, you can have a great men's ministry, even in a small church. You don't have to be a "megachurch" with a pastoral staff of twenty and a budget of 4 million dollars to have quality, needs-based, and effective men's ministry.

Let's look at some of the resources available and then look at ideas for using them.

Resource Review

Imported Seminars

Dad's University is the brainchild of Paul Lewis, creator of the *Dad's Only* newsletter (*see* pages 225 and 226). It is a proven strategy for regularly attracting new men to your church and for helping every dad be a successful father.

Dad's U offers a balanced fathering curriculum of eight half-day courses that equip fathers and energize outreach to un-churched men. They are taught by certified instructors based all over America. The basic idea is that you offer one half-day course every six to twelve months. After each course, "Trax Teams" form . . . small groups that meet regularly for encouragement, accountability, and further input. Dad's U provides ample follow-up materials to provide enrichment for the Trax Teams. (The monthly *Dad Trax* audiocassette resource for fathering discussions is the reason for the name "Trax Team.")

It's easy to get excited when you look at their course descriptions:

* "Secrets of Fast-Track Fathering" explores the power of fathering, balancing career and family priorities, avoiding eight common fathering mistakes, drug-proofing children, and shaping one's fathering legacy.

* "Discovering Your Fathering Design" uses the *Personal Fathering Profile* instrument to identify a man's own fathering style and to explore the key factors and dimensions of successful and satisfying fathering.

* "The Seven Keys to Successful Kids" teaches the parenting techniques that enable one's children to grow into mature and capable adults.

* "Discovering Your Child's Genius" equips a dad to identify and work with the unique personality and learning style of each of his children.

* "The Power of Team Parenting" explores practical techniques for making a strong marriage the foundation for effective fathering.

* "Kids and the Joy of Work" uncovers the deep meaning of work in life, how to choose work that is fulfilling, and how one's children learn a balanced and effective work ethic.

* "Raising Money-Savvy Children" unfolds the dynamics of

family money, debt management, budgeting techniques, and ways to assure one's children will manage money wisely.

  * "Preparing Confident Kids for a Bonkers World" shows fathers how to give children the thinking skills for making wise life choices throughout the twenty-first century, including the value of helping others.

I think you can see how these topics can make fathering the basis for a broad-based men's ministry.

For more information about this exciting outreach and growth ministry contact:

> Dad's University
> P. O. Box 270616
> San Diego, CA 92198-1616
> 619-487-0891

Dad, the Family Shepherd is led by Dave Simmons. His organization offers a Friday-evening/all-day Saturday seminar designed to give dads a strong biblical understanding of their roles as father, husband, and provider. Almost 80 percent of the men who attend the seminar become involved in "E Teams" accountability groups that are set up following the seminar. Smaller churches can elect to go through the seminar by videotape (no minimum attendance); larger groups should plan one year in advance for a speaker to conduct the seminar (three hundred minimum attendance). Contact:

> Dad, the Family Shepherd
> Reg Hamman
> P.O. Box 21445
> Little Rock, AR 72221
> 800-234-3237

Building Strong Families is led by Steve Farrar. Steve's dynamic seminar centers on the man's role in the family as husband and father. The seminar is for both husbands and wives. His experience is that a wife better supports her husband as a father if she, as well as he, receives the input. Steve is the author of *Point Man: How a Man Can Lead a Family* (Multnomah, 1990) and has an earned doctorate from Dallas Theological Seminary. His enthusiasm and insight about fathering come through loud and clear. A video version of the seminar is also available. Contact:

> Strategic Living
> P.O. Box 8333
> Douglas Avenue, Suite 950 LB 22
> Dallas, TX 75225
> 214-361-5511

On Video

In addition to the video versions of the seminars above, *see What Dads Need to Know About Fathering* by James Dobson. It includes one videotape and a leader's guide and is set up for two one-hour learning sessions or one two-hour session. This is available for rental from many Christian bookstores or may be purchased from:

> Focus on the Family
> 420 North Cascade Avenue
> Colorado Springs, CO 80903
> 719-531-3400

Books With Discussion Questions

These are available at your local Christian bookstore or directly from the publishers.

Delivering the Male (Out of the Tough Guy Trap) by Clayton Barbeau (Harper & Row, 1982).
Forever a Father, Always a Son . . . Discovering the Difference a Dad Can Make by Charles William (Victor Books, 1991).
Man in the Mirror . . . Solving the 24 Problems Men Face by Patrick Morely (Wolgemuth & Hyatt, 1989).

Temptations Men Face . . . Straightforward Talk on Power, Money, Affairs, Perfectionism, Insensitivity by Tom Eisenman (InterVarsity Press, 1990).

Books Without Discussion Questions

These books are available at Christian bookstores or directly from the publishers.

Action Plan for Great Dads by Gordon MacDonald (Tyndale House, 1986).

How to Be a Good Dad by Stephen Bly (Moody Press, 1986).

Maximized Manhood: A Guide to Family Survival by Edwin Cole (P.O. Box 610588, Dallas, Texas, 75261).

Point Man: How a Man Can Lead a Family by Steve Farrar (Multnomah, 1990).

Things We Wish We Had Said: Reflections of a Father and His Grown Son by Tony and Bart Campolo (Word Books, 1989).

Recommended Secular Books On Fathering

The following books are available at or through bookstores everywhere.

Between Father and Child: How to Become the Kind of Father You Want to Be by Ronald Levant and John Kelly (Penguin Books, 1989).

How to Father by Fitzhugh Dodson (Signet, 1972).

Fatherhood by Bill Cosby (Berkeley, 1986).

Magazines/Newsletters

Dad's Only . . . News and Creative Ideas for Christian Dads and Husbands. Six bimonthly issues for $24.00, which also includes two *Dad Trax* audiocassettes. Each eight-page newsletter features the best tips, creative ideas, and practical research available on fathering, child development, marriage, and family. Write:

> P.O. Box 270616
> San Diego, CA 92198-1616
> 619-487-0891

Parents of Teenagers, published by Group Publishers. A one-year subscription is $18.97 for six issues. Write:

> P.O. Box 481
> Loveland, CO 80539
> 303-669-3836

Booklets Available From Focus on the Family

Suggested donation is $.35 each. Write:

> Focus on the Family
> 420 North Cascade Avenue
> Colorado Springs, CO 80903
> 719-531-3400

Busy Husbands, Lonely Wives by James Dobson
Chuck Swindoll Talks About Fatherhood by Chuck Swindoll
Help for the Workaholic and His Family by various authors
How To Be a Caring Dad by Stephen Bly
The Loving Leader: A Man's Role at Home by Dean Merrill
Taking Time Out To Be Dad by Wilson W. Grant
Thirty Ideas for Husbands and Fathers by Paul Lewis

Customizing a Plan for Your Church

It's an old adage, right? "Fail to plan, and you plan to fail." Ministry to fathers in our churches won't happen automatically. Pastors and concerned laymen can set goals of encouragement and outreach and lay out a plan.

From the resources above, what are some possible approaches to a ministry to fathers?

Import a Seminar

Do this every year, or sign up with Dad's University. Advantages include the acknowledged expertise of the person you are bringing in to speak and the attention the event receives because it is so special.

Fatherhood From the Pulpit

As we saw in chapter 3, there are many good and not-so-good fathers in the Bible. They make excellent sermon material. One church I know has a "Focus on Fathers" night in their evening service. When this is done, ten dads answer questions such as, (1) what is a challenge I am currently facing as a father and (2) what is one verse of Scripture that encourages me as a Christian dad? The pastor then gives a brief presentation, using a chapter from one of the books mentioned above. Asking ten men to participate in advance, and publicizing that these men will be speaking, serves to interest other men in attending. It's hard to lose using this approach.

"Being a Better Dad" Sunday-School Classes

Depending on the size of your church, a three-month-long class could be held annually or in alternating years. You do not need a resident expert to make this class a success. Get a men's book that includes discussion questions. Each man reads a chapter or section each week. The class leader summarizes the chapter's contents each week, taking only ten minutes. Then the class divides into small groups and works through the questions at the end of the chapter. Choose a book that uses Scripture in the discussion-question section, and you will have a built-in Bible study. Each small group then closes with supportive prayer for one another. As you have no doubt noticed by now, this book is designed with exactly this format in mind, and the thirteen chapters fit with a thirteen-week Sunday quarter.

A big advantage of using this idea is that men must process the material with other men and reveal what they intend to do about the insights they are gaining.

Special Seminars

Instead of importing a prepackaged outside seminar, design your own. Make it a monthly meeting, a Saturday-morning quarterly, or whenever is best. Use the books listed as a resource, and choose topics that are most relevant to the men in your church. Customize it even further by having a session for dads with preschoolers, dads with elementary-age kids, and so on. Be sure to allow time for them to compare notes on their experiences. They will really enjoy hearing from one another. Anytime you target a "special needs" group of fathers, be sure to allow this time for just talking with each other.

This seminar may not have the polish of the big-gun/nationally famous speakers, but you can design your seminars to fit the exact needs of your men. The expense is nil unless you have them each purchase the book you are using yourself as a resource.

Dad's Night Out Socials With the Kids

Father-son or father-daughter events can be a real highlight. One church I know planned an event for dads and their junior-high-age sons: attending a major league baseball game. The junior-high girls, however, rose up in indignation, so it became a father-son, father-daughter event. What is fun and available in your area? It's not hard to organize this kind of event. Fathers who are not accustomed to one-on-one time with their kids may find this an important first step.

Small Groups

Mentioned above many times already, this is where solid changes begin to occur. If a man knows he is going to give an account to four good friends next Saturday morning about his anger problem with the kids, chances are he will actually improve.

Try this: Promote men's small groups as a six-week limited time commitment. To be in a group, a man must commit to come regularly, but the commitment lasts only the six weeks. You will find many groups will not want to disband but keep right on meeting when the official time limit expires. Provide a book that has discussion questions at the end of each chapter, and no "resident expert" needs to lead the group.

Fathering Resource Center

Men are not famous for browsing through Christian bookstores or the sometimes dusty shelves of church libraries. Bring together videos, audiocassettes, books, pamphlets—anything especially geared toward men. Give these resources a special spot in the library, and draw attention to it from the pulpit and by an attractive display. Once a quarter, have a man give a three-minute resource review or testimony as to how a video, tape, or book has been an encouragement.

Target Group Ministry

This is an ongoing small group for fathers who share a special need. What needs would motivate a man to join a special small group? (1) Fathers whose kids are prodigal will bring men (and women) together to share, cry, and pray. (2) Physically handicapped children can require such herculean efforts of the father that he will join a group.

Counseling

Many large churches have full- or part-time counselors as part of the pastoral staff. Make sure one has a specialty in male/husband/father issues. A congregation can be taught that seeking professional help is a sign of strength, not weakness.

A Sneaky Way to Get Every Father, in Time, in Touch With Resources

Resources are wonderful, but many men just won't take the time to find out what is available and then get learning. Assuming your church can't afford to buy every father a subscription to *Dad's Only* ($15.00 per subscription on a group sign-up basis), do it this way: your Sunday school keeps good records of children as they grow up, right? Every year, give every father of a new two-year-old child a subscription to *Dad's Only* or some other fathering resource. Many will renew their subscriptions on their own at the end of their free year. This way, over time, excellent resources can be introduced to all the fathers in your church at only a nominal cost per year.

Remember my opening story in chapter 1? Wow, I was so relieved to give those foster babies back to the social worker! It was hard not to want to give our own daughter back a few months after her screaming entrance into the world. I'm awfully glad I didn't! That same girl is ready for high school now, and her two sisters are just a few years behind. I have learned, sometimes with such dull-brained slowness it is astounding, how to make a little progress toward being a better dad. Through the whole process, these words from the Word continue to be an encouragement:

Now to him who is able to do immeasurably more than all we ask or imagine, according to his power that is at work within us, to him be glory in the church and in Christ Jesus throughout all generations, for ever and ever! Amen.

Ephesians 3:20, 21

God grant us by His Grace that "immeasurably more" we need to be fathers in this difficult day.

Questions for Discussion

1.   Which of the ideas listed in this chapter (or others) is your church now using to help fathers?

2.   Which of the ideas do you think would be most workable for the church you are in? What is the logical next step, then, to make this idea happen?

3.   Look through the Questions for Discussion at the end of each chapter, noticing the Scriptures referenced. Which of these passages of Scripture has been the most significant for you?

Idea Corner 13

With Preschoolers

Teach your kids about another culture, and have some fun at the same time. Play "restaurant" by decorating an area as a certain county. Dress up as a waiter from that country and serve an appropriate food item. Visit your local library for records, tapes, or CDs of that country's music. Your three-year-old will stare at you in wide-eyed amazement when you come dancing in as a Spanish bullfighter!

With Elementary Age

Pick or buy some flowers, and deliver them to some of the shut-ins and senior citizens of your church. If you don't know who they are, ask your pastor. Be prepared to stay and visit for a while. They will enjoy your visit, and you will find senior citizens are like living storybooks. Help your son or daughter know what questions to ask an older person: Where were you born? How many children did you have? What were you doing during World War II? How has our town or city changed since you have lived here? What was school like when you were a child?

With Teenagers

If your town has a soup kitchen, a food bank, or a nursing home, volunteer to help there with your teenager. Visit one place several times, then volunteer at another for a period of time. Compare the needs of people, how we feel when we help those needs, and how this helps us get a perspective on our own lives and health.

Source Notes

Chapter 1 Being a Man Today

1. Michael Lamb, ed., *The Father's Role* (Hillsdale, New Jersey: Lawrence Erlbaum Associates, 1987), 8.

2. Ibid., 10, and Charlie Lewis and Margaret O'Brien, *Reassessing Fatherhood* (Beverly Hills: Sage Publications, Inc., 1987), 67, 68.

3. Lamb, *Father's Role*, 20.

4. Phyllis Bronstein and Carolyn Cowen, *Fatherhood Today* (New York: Wiley & Sons, 1988), 278.

5. Shirley Hanson and Frederick Bozett, *Dimensions of Fatherhood* (New York: Sage Publications, Inc., 1985) 159.

6. Karen Levine, "Are Dads Doing More?" *Parents*, June 1989, 73.

7. Ibid., 76.

8. *Seventeen*, January 1991, 92.

9. Ibid., 93.

10. Ibid., 92.

11. Lewis and O'Brien, *Reassessing,* 39.

12. Earl Grollman and Gerri Sweder, *The Working Parent Dilemma* (Boston: Beacon Press, 1986), 14.

13. James Dobson, *Parenting Isn't for Cowards* (Waco, Texas: Word Books, 1987), 13.

Chapter 2 So Just What Is a Good Dad?

1. Howard Hendricks, *Teaching to Change Lives* (Portland, Oregon: Multnomah Press, 1987), 27.

2. One of the best resources for a deeper explanation of this approach to the Christian life is Watchman Nee's *The Normal Christian Life* (London: Victory Press, 1957).

3. For more information, *see* Len Kageler, *A Youth Minister's Survival Guide: How to Recognize and Overcome the Obstacles You Will Face* (Grand Rapids, Michigan: Zondervan Publishing House, 1992).

4. Barbara Risman and Pepper Schwartz, eds., *Gender in Intimate Relationships* (Belmont, California: Wadsworth Publishing Company, 1989), 221.

5. Cited by Blayne Cutler, "Man of the 90's," *American Demographics,* October 1990, 18.

6. Ibid.

Chapter 3 *Fathers in the Word*

1. Tony and Bart Campolo, *Things We Wish We Had Said* (Dallas: Word Books, 1989), 158.

2. For further discussion, *see* an excellent article by Youth With a Mission's John Dawson, "The Father Heart of God," *The Last Days Newsletter,* Vol. 6, #1, January/February 1983, 16ff.

3. For more biblical information about the fatherhood of God and God as our Father, tour these representative verses: Hosea 11:1; Deuteronomy 14:1; 2 Samuel 7:14; Psalms 2:7, 89:26; Matthew 5:45; John 8:42, 14:6; Galatians 3:16; Romans 8:15, 17, 29; Matthew 6:32.

4. Material in this section is adapted from Len Kageler, *Teen Shaping: Solving the Discipline Dilemma* (Old Tappan, New Jersey: Fleming H. Revell Company, 1990), 27–32.

Chapter 4 *Famous and Infamous Fathers of the Past*

1. Steven Ozment, *When Fathers Ruled: Family Life in Reformation Europe* (Cambridge, Massachusetts: Harvard University Press, 1983), 1.

2. Ibid., 4.

3. Ibid., 147.

4. Ibid., 149.

5. Louise Vernon, *Thunderstorm in Church* (Scottdale, Pennsylvania: Herald Press, 1974), 13.

6. Faith Bailey, *George Mueller: Young Rebel in Bristol* (Chicago: Moody Press, 1958), 125.

7. Faith Bailey, *D.L. Moody: The Valley and the World* (Chicago: Moody Press), 86.

8. For a full discussion of how different parenting styles affect different types of kids, *see* Len Kageler, *Teen Shaping: Solving the Discipline Dilemma* (Old Tappan, New Jersey: Fleming H. Revell Company, 1990).

9. Arthur Marx, *Son of Groucho* (New York: David McKay, 1972).

10. Ibid., 56.

11. Ibid., 70, 71.

Chapter 5 Real Men, Real Struggle

1. *The Growing Child* newsletter can be obtained through Purdue University, West Lafayette, Indiana 47907.

2. Tony and Bart Campolo, *Things We Wish We Had Said* (Dallas: Word Books, 1989), 206.

3. Ibid., 141.

4. Ibid., 155.

5. Bill Cosby, *Fatherhood* (New York: Berkley Publishing Group, 1986).

6. Ibid., 16.

7. Ibid., 52.

8. Ibid., 95.

9. Ibid., 61.

10. Rolf Zettersten, *Turning Hearts Toward Home* (Dallas: Word Books, 1989), 96.

11. Ibid., 69, 70.

Chapter 6 Planned Fatherhood

1. Phyllis Bronstein & Carolyn Cowen, *Fatherhood Today* (New York: Wiley & Sons, 1988), 278.

2. Fitzhugh Dodson, *How to Father* (New York: Penguin Books, 1975), 200.

3. Stephan A. Small, "Toward a Multidimensional Assessment of Work Spillover Into Family Life," *Journal of Marriage and Family*, Vol. 52, February 1990, 51.

4. Paul Thorne, "The Switched Off Executive Is a Leisure Time Dropout," *International Management*, Vol. 43, July-August 1988, 65.

5. Neal Peirce, "Where Are the Children?" *The Seattle Times*, March 27, 1991, A17.

6. Patrick Morely, *The Man in the Mirror* (Brentwood, Tennessee: Wolgemuth & Hyatt, 1989), 6.

7. Ibid., 9.

8. Amy Saltzman, *Downshifting* (New York: HarperCollins, 1991).

9. Blayne Cutler, "Where Does the Free Time Go?" *American Demographics*, November 1990, 38.

Chapter 7 Passing The Torch

1. Les Whitbeck and Viktor Gecas, "Value Attributions and Value Transmissions Between Parent and Child," *Journal of Marriage and the Family*, Vol. 50, August 1988, 829.

2. Bob Laurent, *Keeping Your Teen in Touch With God* (Elgin, Illinois: David C. Cook Publishing Company, 1988), 12.

3. Adapted from Len Kageler, *Helping Your Teenager Cope With Peer Pressure* (Loveland, Colorado: Family Tree of Group Publishers, 1989), 157–162.

4. Ronald Hutchcraft, "Self-Esteem in the Long Run," in *Parents and Teenagers*, Jay Kesler with Ronald Beers, eds. (Wheaton, Illinois: Victor Books, 1984), 292, 293.

5. Based on James Dobson, *Hide or Seek* (Old Tappan, New Jersey: Fleming H. Revell Company, 1974), chapter 4.

6. Kageler, *Helping*, 167–169.

Chapter 8 Special Considerations 1

1. Nicky Marone, *How to Father a Successful Daughter* (New York: McGraw-Hill, Inc., 1988), 3, 4. Used by permission.

2. Ibid., 72.

3. Carey Quan Gelernter, "Want Some Time With Dad? Better Call Ahead" *The Seattle Times*, May 29, 1991, F-1, citing a national study by Diane Lye, sociologist at the University of Washington.

4. David Macaulay *The Way Things Work* (Boston: Houghton Mifflin Company, 1988).

5. Lee Salk, *My Father, My Son* (New York: Putnam Publishing Group, 1982).

6. For a fuller presentation of this concept, *see* Lewis Yablonsky, *Fathers & Sons* (New York: Simon & Schuster, Inc., 1982), 89ff.

7. Steve Farrar, *Point Man: How a Man Can Lead a Family* (Portland, Oregon: Multnomah Press, 1990), 236–240.

8. As listed in "Word Watch" by Ann Soukhanov, *The Atlantic*, Vol. 259, #9, May 1987, 100.

Chapter 9 Special Considerations 2

1. "The June Almanac," *The Atlantic*, Vol. 267, #6, June 1991, 16.

2. For a much fuller presentation of these parenting styles, *see* Kathleen S. Berger, *The Developing Person Through Childhood and Adolescence* (New York: Worth Publishers, 1986), 531. *See also* my own book *Teen Shaping*, where an entire chapter is given to illustrating and accounting for these parenting styles. The Style of Parenting Questionnaire is also included and explained on 43–45.

3. Peter Benson and Dorothy Williams, *The Quicksilver Years* (San Francisco: Harper & Row, 1987), 195.

4. Dorothy Rogers, *Adolescence and Youth*, 5th ed. (Englewood Cliffs, New Jersey: Prentice Hall, 1985), 244.

5. Benson and Williams, *Quicksilver Years*, 187.

6. Ibid., 195.

7. Robert Ailes, *You Are the Message* (Homewood, Illinois: Dow Jones-Irwin, 1988), 3.

8. Fitzhugh Dodson, *How to Single Parent* (New York: Harper & Row, 1987), 3.

9. Ibid., adapted 44, 48, 50.

10. Ronald Levant and John Kelly, *Between Father and Child* (New York: Viking Penguin, 1989), 203.

11. Elizabeth Carter and Monica McGoldrick, *The Changing Family Life Cycle,* 2nd ed. (New York: Gardner Press, 1988), 346.

Chapter 10 The Wounded Father

1. James Dobson, *Parenting Isn't for Cowards,* (Waco, Texas: Word Books, 1987), 42.

2. Ibid., 36, 39.

3. John Wesley White, *Parents in Pain* (Downers Grove, Illinois: InterVarsity Press, 1979), 105.

4. Ibid.

5. Gordon MacDonald, *Rebuilding Your Broken World* (Nashville: Thomas Nelson, 1988), 153, 163, 172.

Chapter 11 The Renewed Father

1. For a full description of this sad scenario, *see* Diane Vaughan's *Uncoupling . . . How Relationships Come Apart* (New York: Vintage Books, 1986).

2. *See The Seattle Times,* June 20, 1991, A-1.

3. Len Kageler, *Teen Shaping: Solving the Discipline Dilemma* (Old Tappan, New Jersey: Fleming H. Revell Company, 1990), 122.

4. Ibid., 123.

5. For a book-length treatment of this concept, *see* Joseph Procaccini and Mark Keifaber, *Parent Burnout* (New York: Doubleday and Company, Inc., 1983).

Chapter 12 How a Wife Can Help Her Husband Be a Better Dad

1. I realize I am portraying massive sexual stereotyping here. I am not defending it, only describing what I see and what other counselors and researchers confirm was the typical gender-identification patterns of our day.

2. Martin Greenberg, *The Birth of a Father* (New York: Continuum Publishing Company, 1985), 144.